"Business schools have become an international business. Professor Peter Lorange has been at the forefront of this internationalization and his experiences at IMD have given him a unique perspective on anticipating the future of global business and designing business schools accordingly. Senior leaders at the top schools will find this to be an insightful and stimulating book."

Thomas S. Robertson, *Dean, Wharton School,*
University of Pennsylvania

"Business schools are often criticized for being out of touch with the profession they were created to serve. At IMD, however, Peter Lorange and his colleagues have created a unique, highly successful business school that is tightly focused on making good managers better. In this fascinating book, Peter explains clearly how IMD works and why it works that way in order to serve professional managers. While the IMD model is not for everyone, this book is a 'must-read' for all who care about the future of business education."

Richard Schmalensee, *Former Dean,*
MIT Sloan School of Management

"This book explains the IMD way regarding executive education and business schools' value creation – our experience of working with IMD has shown this to be a powerful and effective approach."

Hugh Mitchell, *Director of Human Resources, Royal Dutch Shell plc*

"Academic leadership is like being an entrepreneur! This is behind Peter Lorange's success in bringing IMD to the forefront. This book will be an inspiration to other academic leaders to also do this."

Muhtar Kent, *President and Chief Operating Officer,*
The Coca-Cola Company

"Under Peter Lorange's leadership over the last 14 years, IMD has become a yet more formidable competitor. 'Business' isn't so much the adjective but the noun when describing the IMD business school. In this straightforward text, Peter lays out how to manage human capital for strategic advantage. In doing so, he gives advice that serves leaders for whom 'business' is the both the adjective and the noun."

Edward A. Snyder, *Dean, Graduate School of Business,*
The University of Chicago

"Nestlé and IMD have had a strong learning partnership for many years. I can personally attest to the value that we have both derived from the knowledge sharing that goes on between our two institutions. This book encapsulates the essence of IMD's winning formula and will be of interest to both academic and business leaders.

Peter Brabeck-Latmathe, *Chairman and CEO, Nestlé*

Thought Leadership Meets Business

For leading corporations, talent is perhaps the only truly sustainable competitive advantage. In light of this, leading international corporations need to be staffed by the best possible executive talent from around the world. This talent revolution places a burden on business schools to offer highly focused learning, based on current and practical research. In addition, business schools face fierce competition in this sector from corporate universities and Asian management education institutions. *Thought Leadership Meets Business* offers significant new insights into the factors that have led to the delivery of high-quality executive education at the top-ranking IMD. Drawing on the experience and wisdom gained by IMD President Peter Lorange over a distinguished career of more than thirty years, this book offers a powerful model for business school success.

This book will be of interest to business school leaders and educators, as well as policy-makers concerned with education.

PETER LORANGE has been president of IMD in Lausanne, Switzerland since 1993. He is Professor of Strategy and holds the Nestlé Chair. He was formerly president of the Norwegian School of Management and, before this, was affiliated to the Wharton School, Pennsylvania. Professor Lorange has written or edited 18 books and some 120 articles on the topics of global strategic management, strategic planning and entrepreneurship for growth.

Thought Leadership Meets Business

How business schools can become more successful

PETER LORANGE
President IMD, The Nestlé Professor

CAMBRIDGE
UNIVERSITY PRESS

CAMBRIDGE UNIVERSITY PRESS

Cambridge, New York, Melbourne, Madrid, Cape Town, Singapore,
São Paulo, Delhi

Cambridge University Press
The Edinburgh Building, Cambridge CB2 8RU, UK

Published in the United States of America by Cambridge University
Press, New York

www.cambridge.org
Information on this title: www.cambridge.org/9780521897228

First published 2008
Reprinted 2008
Printed in the United Kingdom at the University Press, Cambridge

A catalogue record for this publication is available from the British
Library

ISBN 978-0-521-89722-8 hardback

Contents

Figures

Tables

Foreword

I served as the dean of the Richard Ivey School of Business in Canada for five years in the 1990s. Like many other deans, I had not sought the position or had it as a career goal. Rather I was approached by the search committee and asked whether I would be willing to serve. I had only a couple of months to do some planning and to put in place the key members of our leadership team.

While being a business school dean shares many elements with other leadership roles, there are unique things about being a leader in an academic institution and, in particular, being a dean in a business school. A business school in a university has quite a complex set of knowledgeable and demanding stakeholders. In taking on the role, I had little relevant codified knowledge and experience to draw on other than my own casual observations and experience as a faculty member. It would have been a Godsend to have been able to benefit from Peter Lorange's thinking and experience as president of IMD.

Peter has been very successful in moving what was a good European business school in the early 1990s to one that is now widely regarded as one of the best in the world, particularly in the area of executive education. With very little growth in faculty numbers, he and the IMD team of faculty and staff have tripled the volume and quintupled the profitability of the institution. I have been fortunate to be a member of the IMD faculty team for about four years and to experience the later stages of this growth and success. While Peter always puts a lot of emphasis on the role of the "IMD team," I am convinced that without Peter's strong leadership, IMD's success would have been much less certain.

From my observations Peter Lorange has a very clear vision of where IMD is going – much better than most presidents or deans and he has been willing to make the tough decisions that have kept IMD very focused on achieving its objectives. He is widely seen as working tirelessly and very effectively at leading and executing IMD's strategy.

While there are certainly major differences in leading IMD to leading a business school in a largely publicly funded university, many of his ideas do have real applicability in that different setting. In my opinion this book is a "must read" for anybody in a leadership role in a business school or any other professional school.

Adrian Ryans
Former dean, Richard Ivey School of Business
and
Professor of Marketing and Strategy, IMD

Preface

I have been involved in executive education for more than thirty years as a teacher, leader and strategist in schools all over the world, including Sloan, Wharton, Norwegian School of Management and IMD. Now, as I approach the next stage of my life, it seems like a good time to crystallize my thoughts on the subject.

In essence, I shall be claiming in this book that the "classic" business school operating model generally seems to be collapsing. I will identify the most important trends in business education that are contributing to this and give the reader food for thought regarding the optimal business model that an academic institution should choose in order to address these trends. While I do not claim to have all the answers on how the business school model should adapt, I do claim that my colleagues and I have developed a reasonably effective model, which uniquely positions IMD to address these trends, and can thus be of more general interest. Throughout the book, I will use examples from my IMD experience to illustrate and substantiate my points. This book will thus be intentionally biased toward and rather explicit in one way of running a school, perhaps in the same way that Sir Richard Branson might be if he were writing about Virgin. I believe the IMD way is a solid one, but even if the reader has no particular interest in IMD or the IMD examples that I provide, it is still worthwhile reading because no practicing manager or business academic can responsibly ignore the changing context for business school education. There are four main reasons for writing this book:

First, it deals with an important topic – executive education that delivers true thought leadership. For leading corporations, talent is perhaps the *only* truly sustainable competitive advantage. In light of this fact, leading international corporations need to be staffed by the best possible executive talent from around the world. Thus, this talent revolution has placed a burden on business schools to offer relevant learning, based on current and practical research, for leading executives-cum-learning partners.* Executive education that delivers true thought leadership has indeed become a key priority for many business schools. Many of these schools, however, fall short of the challenge to meet today's executive education needs. Classic organizational structures – often based on functional disciplines, hierarchy and the tenure tradition – can impede a business school's ability to adapt quickly to the new and emerging requirements of leading corporations. Many business school professors and leaders, as well as the administrative staff that support them, feel the conflict between the "old" ways of creating academic value, based on disciplines and set axioms, and the "new" ways of creating academic value, where professors and practitioners work together in a give-and-take mode, as learning partners. However, it is probably the new mode of academic value-creation – a "lead *and* be led" mode – that is the most likely to prevail. If so, this will have a profound impact on how the business school of the future is organized and managed.

Second, there is a shift taking place in global economic power, and this, too, will likely have an enormous impact on business schools. Traditionally, the locus of economic wealth creation has been in the West – the United States and Europe. Much of the common knowledge taught in business schools can be traced back to business practices from these areas. Today, however, the locus of economic growth has shifted to Asia. Japan has long been the second-largest economy (in terms of GNP) in the world. China is

---

* The term "learning partner" is used quite extensively throughout this book in place of students, participants, sponsoring companies and clients. We have chosen this term because we believe that two-way partnerships lead to the most effective learning. For the sake of simplicity, however, we have sometimes referred to our learning partners as students, participants, sponsoring companies and clients. While these terms can signal a one-way relationship where the business school's agenda is imposed, this is not in line with the key messages in this book. When we use these terms we are thinking of them as learning partners.

increasingly playing a more prominent role, and India and Southeast Asia are on the rise. But are the theories being taught in most business schools reflecting this shift and its underlying paradigms? The answer is no. Most business schools are still researching and teaching "Western" business practices. However, we expect that Asian-rooted business paradigms and thought leadership will become relatively much more prominent. This book discusses how business schools might cope with this challenge.

Third, to the best of my knowledge, this book is conceptually sound and relatively well tested. I have had the benefit of being the president of IMD for the last fifteen years. Before that, I was the president of the Norwegian School of Management for four years, and department head at the Wharton School and head of both the Lauder Institute and the William H. Wurster Center for International Management Studies – at the University of Pennsylvania – for several years. My experiences in all of these roles constitute the "testing ground" for this book. One limitation is that the book is based primarily on my own experiences – that is, it is not empirically tested *per se*. However, it is important to recognize that this thirty-plus-year journey represents the type of incremental, scientific insight building that I am proposing throughout this book. Above all, over time, I have brought various thought leadership themes to the table, which then became the basis for dialogue with leading practitioners, who in turn shared their insights regarding how business schools should be run. For me, the book represents an evolution in my thinking. At Wharton, as chairman of the Management Department, I attempted to bring academics from several disciplines together, in effect to create a more cross-disciplinary, less department-based structure. I realized then that this can be both difficult and less than stable. At the Lauder Institute, which I chaired for two years, we created an alternative to Wharton's main MBA program, which had more of an international focus and which enabled us to introduce the humanities, language and political science into the curriculum – the Lauder students were, in fact, awarded both an MBA and an MA degree! At the Wurster Center for International Business Research, which I chaired for three years, we attempted to foster cross-functional research in the arena of international business.

All of these experiences were valuable for me when it came to my ability to handle the position of president at one of Europe's largest business schools, BI–Norwegian School of Management. Here, it became apparent that market segmentation was key. More emphasis was thus put on executive education. BI also went through several mergers – and one of the key things I learned from that experience was that it is more important to emphasize the building of diverse strengths – rather than to create "winners" and "losers."

My experiences at both Wharton and BI were of relevance to me in my role as president of IMD. They represented experiences that I could build on!

Fourth, this book has the strong potential for implementation. As well as outlining key implications for business schools, there are frequent practical examples from IMD – how we make things happen at this institution. Hopefully, this will aid individual readers in implementing solutions to the wide array of key issues they might see in their own institutions. Clearly, this would apply to leaders of business schools, as well as their staff. It may also have implications for the implementation of sounder learning strategies at corporate universities.

In 2002, one of my books, called *New Vision for Management Education: Leadership Challenges* (2002), was published. The present book is largely consistent with what I wrote then, although it represents a significant set of evolutionary developments, particularly when it comes to better understanding the critical role of research and the interplay between practical research and the learning going on with leading business partners.

I have also written a number of articles over the last few years, touching upon several issues relating to academic leadership. The most relevant ones are listed in Appendix II, with short paragraphs covering the essence of the content. While this book draws on several of these articles, some of them rather heavily, it is not a republication of existing articles. The content is largely original.

The target group for the book certainly includes business school leaders, but it is broader than this. University administrators as well as public policy-makers might also find the book of interest. Fundamentally, however, the book is also for all those who are responsible for people development in business – i.e., those who play roles as *partners* with business schools when it comes to people development agendas.

Let me cite finally a crisp, minimalistic philosophical statement from BIC, the Paris, France, based multinational that is active in various consumer products: "Honor the past – invent the future." Jim Collins, in *Good to great* (2001), cites several companies that have adopted analogous philosophical statements. This stresses that one should try to see the value in what has been good in the past, so as to build on this for the future. This seems to me to be particularly critical when an organization is going through a leadership transition, which is the situation at IMD today.

BOOK OUTLINE

The book starts, in Chapter 1, by laying down the conceptual framework and then placing this in context by looking briefly at how business schools originated and evolved. In Chapter 2, we will examine the key elements that make an executive program an excellent experience for learning partners. Specifically, we will apply this to open and in-company programs as well as to MBA programs. In Chapter 3, we shall delve further into the critical role of research as a key driver for the type of academic value-creation we have proposed. Chapter 4 looks at the marketing activities a business school can undertake to reflect an institution's commitment to two-way academic value-creation. Chapters 5 and 6 then go on to explore how business schools can develop institutional learning and a strategic human resources plan to ensure continuous intellectual growth and institutional learning for the benefit of all – academics and learning partners. In Chapter 7, we focus on the firm and its role in the learning partnership. Throughout the book, we see the importance of strong, professional, proactive leaders at the helms of business schools – as discussed in Chapters 1 through 6 – and also at the helm of corporations – as discussed in Chapter 7. The leadership tasks required for a business school will be discussed in more detail in Chapter 8. Finally, Chapter 9 summarizes what we see as the key success factors for business schools, the factors that perhaps have also brought IMD and its learning partners some success.

In order to drive home the key messages in this book, it is intentionally quite repetitive in places. And, as mentioned, there is a strong bias toward IMD, which I believe is a strength of the book. IMD is unique amongst most business schools, yet it has still been successful, which hopefully makes this case-based story a worthwhile one to tell. Throughout the book, I have attempted to generalize and state some implications. Some readers, however, might ask what they can take away from this. My sense is that, in the end, it will be up to each individual reader to reflect on what has been described and to translate the implications to their own situation, based on their own constraints.

ACKNOWLEDGMENTS

Many people should be thanked for contributing to the insights outlined in this book. I am particularly grateful to IMD's faculty for their continuing support, their exceptionally strong commitment to thought leadership and their continued willingness to engage in positive debate around how "good can be done even better." I have had the privilege of working closely with James Ellert, senior associate dean of IMD, for the past eleven years. He has taught me a lot and I am highly indebted to him. Knut Haanes, Walter Kuemmerle, Daniel Muzyka, Johan Roos and Adrian Ryans provided helpful comments on an earlier version of the manuscript. Beverley Lennox provided important inputs for the first draft of this book, based on the various articles listed in Appendix II, several presentations I have given and face-to-face discussions. She has also rewritten the manuscript based on my extensive inputs. Thank you for a good job, Bev! Lindsay McTeague has edited the manuscript, also in an outstanding manner. Eva Ferrari and Annette Polzer have done a lot of transcribing and typing. I am most thankful to all of the above for their inputs, support and encouragement.

I Background and conceptual framework

> I think the biggest issue and opportunity is globalization. As business becomes more global, and our students and faculty more international, we need to build on the efforts we've launched and seek new ways to prepare students to lead in a globalized world.
>
> Jay Light, dean, Harvard Business School[1]

KEY POINTS

- The growth and complexity of businesses today is spurring strong growth and fierce competition in the executive education segment.[2]
- Companies and executives want development opportunities that are grounded in real life.
- In order to maximize academic value, business schools must adopt an interactive, two-way learning approach where propositional knowledge meets prescriptive knowledge.
- This interactive, two-way learning partnership benefits all involved – practitioners and professors alike.

INTRODUCTION

The challenge for business schools is to create value for their learning partners by establishing the critical link between real-life issues and

---

[1] As quoted in R. Thompson, "Light years ahead," *HBS Alumni Bulletin* (September 2006).

[2] See, for instance, R. Khurana, *From higher aims to hired hands: The social transformation of American business schools and the unfulfilled promise of management as a profession* (Princeton: Princeton University Press, 2007); T. Durand and S. Dameron, *The future of business schools, scenarios and strategies for 2020* (Basingstoke: Palgrave Macmillan, forthcoming); R. Gupta, S. Tomar and S. Sharma, "Challenges for management education: Evolving strategies for low end B-schools," *Journal of Educational Planning and Administration*, 10, 3 (July 2006), 321–332. See also E. F. Gay, "The founding of the Harvard Business School," *Harvard Business Review* 4 (1927), 397–400.

research-based management insights. While this viewpoint may be quite commonplace nowadays, it is still rare to find schools that do it well. Too often, even those schools with the best intentions have failed to translate their ambitions into action. They frequently treat the teaching of executives as a one-way process, talking "to them" rather than "with them." They have not grasped how to deliver their research findings in more meaningful and interesting ways so that practicing managers can internalize them and apply them to their real-world situations. And they do not see the critical two-way link between research and teaching where academics and learning partners enrich one another's understanding – one must "lead *and* be led,"[3] be "in front of the cart *and* behind it!" This applies to academics and practitioners alike.

The growth and unparalleled complexity that businesses are experiencing today will undoubtedly continue to stimulate strong growth and fierce competition in the executive education segment. In order to meet the needs of business and remain competitive in the marketplace, it will be critical for business schools to adopt a strategy that links research and teaching in such a way that the academic value is maximized for all sides of the learning partnership. As Lars Engwall, a renowned professor and researcher at Uppsala University in Sweden, and a leading scholar on the historical development of business schools, states,

> It should be evident . . . that management education could be considered a growth industry globally. It has been stimulated by the economic development since industrialization, and the following emergence of complex organizations with increasing needs to coordinate physical and financial flows in an effective way. It has also been part of a general tendency in many countries to increase the ratio of the population with academic degrees. In this process, management education has had the

---

[3] N. Kumar, L. Scheer and P. Kotler, "From market driven to market driving," *European Management Journal* 18 (2000), 129.

advantage to be relatively cheap, in comparison to programs in engineering, medicine, etc. It has also been attractive to students, since it offers wide opportunities for employment. Management concepts have even been spreading to such an extent that they are used in various contexts in the professional as well as the private lives of modern individuals.[4]

The tremendous thirst for management concepts is evidenced by the huge growth in popular business books over the last two or three decades. While managers have become much more empowered by the information and opportunities available to them, many business schools have not kept pace. This raises some fundamental questions that this book attempts to address:

- How can research and learning in the classroom come closer together? How can the *speed* of research findings going into the classroom be improved?
- How can a more innovative culture be created in today's business schools? This could include learning from modern corporations such as IBM, 3M, Procter & Gamble and others!
- How can we break down conservative barriers in order to stimulate more experimentation so that the business school's value proposition can be continually strengthened – "making good even better"?

Some scholars have argued that business schools are too often intellectually shallow.[5] Khurana, for instance, has undertaken a comprehensive study of the evolution of American business schools.[6] He

---

[4] L. Engwall, "The anatomy of management education," *Scandinavian Journal of Management* 23 (March 2007), 4–35.

[5] R. A. Gordon and J. E. Howell, *Higher education for business* (New York: Columbia University Press, 1959); H. Mintzberg, *Managers, not MBAs: A hard look at the soft practice of managing and management development* (San Francisco, CA: Berrett-Koehler Publishers, 2004).

[6] R. Khurana, *From higher aims to hired hands: The social transformation of American business schools and the unfulfilled promise of management as a profession* (Princeton, NJ: Princeton University Press, 2007).

feels that the strong focus on the MBA students-cum-customers, found in many business schools today, has led to too much emphasis on how to maximize short-term economic success for these students. He argues that the more fundamental intellectual and moral training of leaders must now be readdressed. The standards of the management profession must be elevated.

Augier and March, in their "The pursuit of relevance in management education," argue that ambiguity and myopia put real constraints on finding relevance. Hence, they argue instead for attempting to find meaning and trying to strive for essence, even beauty.[7] When business schools become too far removed from real-life practice, they conflict with the day-to-day reality of managing, and this leads to irrelevance and even, as some have argued, the destruction of good managerial practice.[8]

CONCEPTUAL FRAMEWORK: CREATING ACADEMIC VALUE

Too focused on "scientific" research, business schools are hiring professors with limited real-world experience and graduating students who are ill equipped to wrangle with complex, unquantifiable issues – in other words, the stuff of management . . . Some of the research produced is excellent, but because so little of it is grounded in actual business practices, the focus of graduate business education has become increasingly circumscribed – and less and less relevant to practitioners.[9]

As the business environment becomes increasingly complex, executives and corporations are becoming more and more demanding. In order to cater to their development needs, business schools must acknowledge that a "learning partnership" approach is far more effec-

---

[7] M. Augier and J. G. March, "The pursuit of relevance in management education," *California Management Review* 49 (Spring 2007), 129–146.

[8] S. Ghoshal, "Bad management theories are destroying good management practices," *IEEE Engineering Management Review* 33 (2005), 79.

[9] W. G. Bennis and J. O'Toole, "How business schools lost their way," *Harvard Business Review* 83 (May 2005), 96–104.

tive than the traditional "we teach you" way of doing things. Therefore, they must adopt a more interactive, two-way learning approach that links research with practice. Why should business schools strive to achieve the critical link between research and real life in the classroom? First, it is a matter of necessity! Second, it is also a matter of further enhancing the level and speed of academic value-creation by building on this two-way link in the classroom. This exchange between professors and state-of-the-art practitioners results in a more rapid progression of insights for all involved than can be achieved through more classic approaches to research.

So how do business schools create academic value in their key academic programs? It is critical that they focus on their learning partners when it comes to setting the research and teaching agenda. They must address the current challenges that companies have to deal with. In doing so, they need to recognize that executives are typically facing multidisciplinary management issues that are, in general, no longer served by the narrow axiomatic research conducted in the more discipline-oriented silos of traditional business schools. At the same time, it is clear that learning partners (the market) come to business schools to "learn the latest" and be "conceptually inspired." Consequently, business schools need to find the right balance between being market driven and conceptually driven. The latter comes via insightful research that brings new and challenging thought leadership to the table.

In his book, *The gifts of Athena*, Joel Mokyr describes two types of knowledge: "propositional" knowledge (the "what") and "prescriptive" knowledge (the "how").[10] Propositional knowledge is focused on understanding and developing basic laws and models. Of course, we realize that in business there are few, if any, definite laws. Instead, the laws in business represent the fundamental truths by which business operates at a particular point in time. Mokyr calls this Ω (omega)

---

[10] J. Mokyr, *The gifts of Athena* (Princeton, NJ: Princeton University Press, 2002).
Please note that Mokyr and his thinking are mentioned many times throughout this book. In each case, these references are to *The gifts of Athena*.

6 THOUGHT LEADERSHIP MEETS BUSINESS

knowledge. For example, the widely tested "five forces" model of Michael Porter – the most influential scholar in the field of strategy over the last three decades – is an example of propositional knowledge.[11] Many of the efforts in academia to add empirical insight fall into the category of propositional knowledge.

Prescriptive knowledge, by contrast, is gained through experiencing, understanding and developing techniques to manage specific situations. It can be found in many "How to . . ." management books by practitioners. In business strategizing, for example, prescriptive knowledge could be illustrated by the saying, "Strategy means choice!" It has not been tested, nor is it testable, but it represents good business practice. Of course, business will always be evolving, and executives will continue to develop new prescriptive knowledge and techniques. Mokyr calls this λ (lambda) knowledge.

According to Mokyr, the interplay between these two types of knowledge – propositional and prescriptive – is essential. They complement each other and the continuous interaction between them sets the stage for positive change. These complementary sources of knowledge – Ω and λ – must meet each other in an iterative process.

In applying Mokyr's thinking to management education, we can see thus that when the two types of knowledge are brought into the classroom – the prescriptive knowledge, primarily by the participants through good practice, and the propositional knowledge, primarily by the faculty through research – they reinforce each other, provided they are introduced at the appropriate time and in the right balance. This approach requires dialogue, as it involves blending new academic knowledge with the tried and tested actions of practicing managers in a dynamically changing world. A give-and-take attitude and the ability to listen and reflect will be key. In reality, managers, as well as faculty, develop propositional knowledge all the time, and they bring this knowledge into the classroom.

---

[11] M. Porter, *Competitive strategy* (New York: The Free Press, 1980).

And faculty, through their consulting, case writing, coaching and facilitating activities, develop prescriptive knowledge. Thus, in reality, *both* managers and professors develop both categories of knowledge, and they must both be mentally set to lead and to be led. This has important implications for teaching and research. To be truly cutting edge, teaching must be research based, with propositional knowledge as part of it – thought leadership! And research must be exposed to strong practicing managers so that the research insights themselves evolve. Indeed, research now takes the form of grounded theory building,[12] i.e. the creation of grounded rationality in a more meaningful way.

While the academic value-creation model we propose – where practical research "meets" the best of practice – will typically be well adapted to executive development program settings, this academic value-creating model could also easily apply to other more traditional academic settings. For MBA programs, for instance, the key would be to develop an eclectic program design and then attempt to attract participants who are more experienced. Even for a PhD program, the approach may have merit as long as such a program has a cross-disciplinary focus rather than the axiomatic bent that these programs usually have. Ideally, the PhD candidates would have a fair amount of managerial experience, again in contrast to the typical PhD student, who is typically young and "right out of school." But, the question in the end would be: Who would hire this breed of doctoral students?

Even when it comes to undergraduate programs, there might be benefits from being inspired by our learning model. For instance, key courses could be cross functional and co-taught by professors with different disciplinary backgrounds. A core course in ethics, for example, might draw on faculty from business, public management, divinity, history and classical philosophy. The students, although typically not

---

[12] B. G. Glaser and A. L. Strauss, *The discovery of grounded theory: Strategies for qualitative research* (Chicago, IL: Aldine, 1967).

as experienced as executives, might come from various genders, backgrounds and nationalities – thus enriching the experience base.

Analogies to Mokyr's proposition regarding intellectual value-generation can also be seen in business practice and business research. New product innovations often seem to come about as a result of interactions with *lead* customers. And the prototype is often improved upon based on the knowledge sharing that takes place between the supplier and the customer. We can find several similar examples in business:

- Procter & Gamble's (P&G) innovation model – Connect and Develop – now accounts for 35 per cent of P&G's innovations. The central idea behind this approach is to use external sources to seek out ideas for new products. According to Huston and Sakkab, both P&G executives, "For most companies, the alternative invent-it-ourselves model is a sure path to diminishing returns."[13]
- Toyota, with its "Toyota way," seems to work with lead customers to develop better products, faster! The company is a master of "Kaisen" – continuous improvement. Barwise and Meehan discuss this in their recent book – *Simply better*.[14] They also have a detailed description of how the Scion, after being launched in the US, was then further improved through a process that involved close interaction with key customer groups. This process enabled Scion to become a great success and the learning was transferred to other brands and launches, notably Lexus and Trundra.[15] Dialogue, give and take, listen and learn have been key factors in Toyota's success.
- At Google, they are fast at generating new products and new ideas and getting fast feedback from their customers to improve them.

---

[13] L. Huston and N. Sakkab, "Connect and develop: Inside Procter & Gamble's new model for innovation – overhaul your approach to innovation, or get out of the race. It's that simple – and that urgent," *Harvard Business Review* 84 (March, 2006), 58.

[14] P. Barwise and S. Meehan, *Simply better: Winning and keeping customers by delivering what matters most* (Boston, MA: Harvard Business School Press, 2004).

[15] P. Barwise and S. Meehan, *Customer insights that matter* (forthcoming).

When there is acceptance of the new product or service, usually after several iterations, it is rolled out on a full scale. Google sees this process as an opportunity to learn rapidly – it is not afraid of failure. As a result, Google is able to come up with an impressive array of innovations, at a rapid pace!

- LEGO is another example of a company that emphasizes customer feedback as part of its innovation model. Devoted LEGO users can design, share and buy their own customized LEGO models through the company's website – factory.lego.com. This has become a strong source for LEGO's product development – and it is particularly effective.

Eric von Hippel and his colleagues may have been the first to come up with the concept that innovations tend to take place by working closely with lead customers, or "lead users" as they call them.[16] More recently, Von Hippel has published his further ideas on "democratizing innovation," where he discusses how lead users develop new products and services for themselves – user-centered innovation.[17] Again, networking with, and listening to, key users can provide valuable new insights!

All of this, taken in the aggregate, is perhaps consistent with Mokyr's thinking and perhaps analogous to the knowledge sharing that goes on at IMD, where tentative new ideas largely from research *meet* a lead group of executives from all over the world. This interaction is central to IMD's academic value-creation.

A BRIEF HISTORY

We can go all the way back to Aristotle, who classified two types of knowledge – knowledge characterized by certainty and precise explanations (e.g. mathematics) and knowledge characterized by probability and imprecise explanations (e.g. human behavior).

---

[16] E. von Hippel, S. Thomke and M. Sonnack, "Creating breakthroughs at 3M," in *Harvard Business Review on Innovation* (Boston, MA: Harvard Business School Press, 2001).

[17] E. von Hippel, *Democratizing innovation* (Cambridge, MA: MIT Press, 2005).

Aristotle did not demand certainty in everything – he emphasized the interplay between the two types of knowledge!

Alternatively, we can adjust our clocks radically forward, and examine the changes that are taking place in how R&D is done in industry, as reported in *The Economist*, on March 1, 2007.[18] There is no longer the split between "R" and "D," no "handover," no dichotomy, but seamless interaction. This new world of research must thus satisfy the consumer, and a short "time-to-market" will enhance downstream innovation. Again – in line with what both Mokyr and Aristotle propose – it is the *interplay* between two phenomena that creates value! Many trends point to this type of interplay – another key point of this book!

But, before continuing, and in order to understand how today's business schools took shape, it may make sense to review their origin briefly along with several important developments along the way. This may shed further light on today's business schools specifically, and academic institutions, such as universities, more generally. The key will be to explore how business schools can build on these developments to create success.

THE TRADITION

The modern university was conceived in 1804 by Alexander von Humboldt, who developed a blueprint for the University of Berlin. This encompassed the creation of functional, discipline-based, axiomatically driven departments, a strong hierarchy of professorial titles, ranks and promotion criteria, and a heavy focus on research, albeit within each specific discipline. Teaching was research-driven in such a way that the discipline-based viewpoints were brought to the classroom by the professor, typically in a one-way exchange, i.e. in what might be characterized as an "inside-out" learning process.[19]

---

[18] "The rise and fall of corporate R&D: Out of the dusty labs," *The Economist* (March 3, 2007).

[19] W. Rüegg (ed.), *A history of the university in Europe*, 3 vols. (Cambridge: Cambridge University Press, 2004), vol. III.

While this innovation was clearly path breaking and of momentous importance in its time, it is perhaps slightly perplexing to observe that many of today's universities – and business schools – are still shaped along similar lines, i.e. highly fragmented within academic departments, extremely hierarchical and with a "teaching *to* the students" mode rather than an approach that incorporates a two-way exchange. Thus, much of what might be seen as weaknesses for many business schools, in terms of limited eclecticism and flexibility, excessive structures, etc., can be traced back to Humboldt's original model. However, the basic commitment to research that he stood for represents the most relevant dimension of his legacy today.

In Walter Rüegg's thoroughly documented history of the university, we can see that before Humboldt's "reform," many universities were much more flexible. They based their academic value-creation on an apprenticeship-type model, where the good professors moved around from university to university, thus spreading innovative ideas more quickly, even many centuries ago![20] Professors were not dependent on a tenure-based, fixed structure. Before the modern university was conceived in the 1800s, universities such as Nalanda in India were attracting prize students and world-renowned faculty from all over Asia more than 1,500 years ago.[21] These were the Oxfords, Cambridges and Harvards of their time. And the initial success of these long-standing academic institutions of excellence, such as Oxford, Cambridge and others, is thus much more similar to the eclectic, non-disciplinary approach that I advocate in this book.

THE MODERN BUSINESS SCHOOL

Nevertheless, Humboldt's design – with its discipline-based departments, axiomatic research within each department, and well-defined hierarchy of academic positions and promotional procedures – has been widely adopted worldwide by universities, including extensively

---

[20] Rüegg (ed.), *A history of the university in Europe*, vol. I.
[21] S. Tharoor, "Reconstructing Nalanda," *The Hindu*, www.hindu.com/thehindu/mag/2006/12/24/stories/2006122400060300.htm (2006), accessed March 27, 2007.

in the US. This is also true for professional schools, such as business schools. While the US has played a formative role in building the modern business school, it has generally been within an organizational framework that can be traced back to Humboldt.

There are perhaps two countries, above all, where the US model has not been widely adopted – France and, paradoxically, Germany. These two countries have come up with alternatives to the US model. In France, there has been a strong cultural and linguistic barrier to the adaptation of the US model. In Germany, the so-called *Handelshochschule*, with the German professional *Lehrstuhls*, have often led to different kinds of highly silo-oriented viewpoints, which have tended to isolate German thinking on business education.

It is clear, however, that the US type of business school organization generally tends to dominate the business school market. As Engwall points out, "The American orientation of management studies has implied an increasing pressure for faculty members to publish their research in international top journals, the latter being defined by their impact. One often used measure for this importance of scholarly journals is the number of times on average an article in a journal is cited."[22] Here, one can see a clear trend toward axiomatic thinking when publishing in well-established journals with a clear disciplinary focus. Of course, one can speculate that this might lead to conservatism because only articles that are relatively "close to the axiomatic norm" might typically be published. As Engwall sums up, "All in all, we can thus conclude that management research and thereby management education has a strong US domination. Top journals are published in the United States, US scholars dominate them and published research – even by non-Americans – is heavily based on earlier US research."

As Howard Thomas, dean of the Warwick Business School in the UK, puts it, "Despite the fact that US schools continue to dominate the global business school landscape (Pfeffer and Fong, 2002), formidable competitors sensitive to local market needs now exist in

---

[22] Engwall, "The anatomy of management education," 4–35.

Europe, Asia and Latin America (Antunes and Thomas, 2006)."[23] Indeed, in this book, I argue extensively for what might be seen as a viable alternative to the traditional US-based organizational form. This is because I believe the traditional, axiomatic, discipline-based research to be less valid than it was before and that the interplay between best practice – the prescriptive knowledge coming from the best firms – and research – the propositional knowledge coming from professors – can give rise to an alternative model for academic value-creation. And this alternative model can perhaps challenge the classical, often US-based, business schools.

Several scholars have indeed observed that business schools can have different organizational forms in various parts of the world. Czarniawska and Sevón,[24] for instance, assume that the US model might be "translated" to other settings. Translation is not the same as duplication! Sahlin-Andersson[25] feels that it will be adapted to new environments, or as Engwall says, "we should note that already the US model has variations. These differences are likely to lead to variations also among followers. In addition, we can anticipate that the transfer of models to other national and cultural contexts will imply adaptation."[26] Thus, there seems to be a growing recognition that there can be several different ways that leading business schools might be organized, all leading to high quality academic value generation.

An important study by the British sociologist Richard Whitley differentiates between academic disciplines.[27] He classifies academic

[23] D. Antunes and H. Thomas, "The competitive (dis)advantages of European business schools," *Long Range Planning* 40 (2007), 382–404. See also H. Thomas, "Business school strategy and the metrics for success," *Journal of Management Development* 26 (2007), 32–42. Included in this reference are references to J. Pfeffer and C. T. Fong, "The end of business schools? Less success than meets the eye," *Academy of Management Learning and Education* 1 (2002), 78–95.

[24] B. Czarniawska and G. Sevón (eds.), *Translating organizational change* (Berlin: De Gruyter, 1996).

[25] K. Sahlin-Andersson, "Imitating by editing success: The construction of organizational fields and identities," in Czarniawska and Sevón (eds.), *Translating organizational change*.

[26] Engwall, "The anatomy of management education," 4–35.

[27] R. D. Whitley, *The intellectual and social organization of the sciences* (Oxford: Oxford University Press, 1984).

disciplines according to functional dependence between researchers and degree of strategic dependence. That is, using my interpretation, he classifies them according to whether there is an eclectic inter-dependence or not, and whether there is a strong, typically shifting, environment-driven evolution in a discipline or not. According to him, the discipline of management has a low degree of functional dependence and a low degree of strategic dependence and he calls this "fragmented ad-hocracy" (p. 158). In my opinion, by contrast, the management discipline should be classified as having *both* high functional dependence between researchers (i.e. eclecticism) *and* a high degree of strategic dependence.

These differences can perhaps be explained by the fact that Whitley's view might be based on a classical, discipline-based, axiomatic view of business research, whereas I feel that business schools should orchestrate the availability of complementary capabilities, allowing for the development of specific propositional knowledge. The discipline of management would thus be labeled "conceptually integrated bureaucracy," according to Whitley's conceptual scheme. This way of characterizing the domain of business research – and business education – would be in contrast to the typical US view of business schools and how they create value.

From my arguments, it definitely follows that attracting and retaining suitable faculty is probably the most critical success factor and the biggest bottleneck for a business school. The bar is even higher for IMD because faculty members need to be generalists and need to be able to do great research *and* teach well. The trend at most business schools is not only the silo-building of academic depart-ments but also toward a fairly dramatic separation of labor; full pro-fessors and tenure-track professors do research, adjunct professors and practitioners teach, and full-time case writers write cases. Clearly, this separation is counterproductive. Case writers do not need to teach the cases they write and thus have less incentive and less insight into how to write suitable cases. Full professors and tenure-track folks are engaged in their own "game," which has little to do

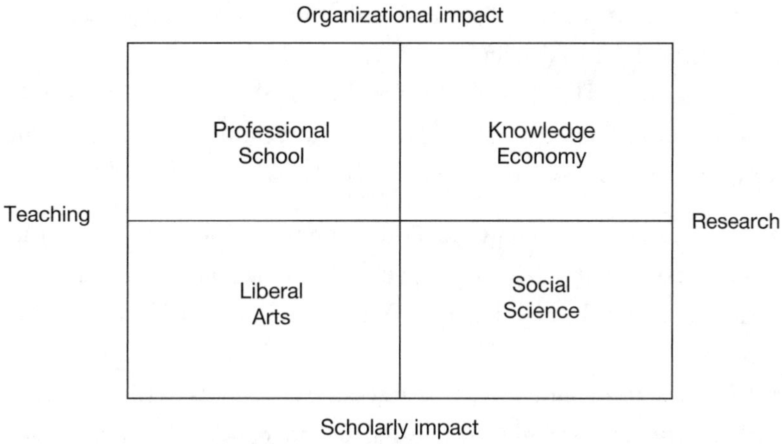

Organizational impact

Professional School	Knowledge Economy
Liberal Arts	Social Science

Teaching ... Research

Scholarly impact

FIGURE 1.1 How a business school's activities might be focused.

Source: C. Ivory, P. Miskell, H. Shipton, A. White, K. Moeslein and A. Neely, *The future of business schools in the UK: Finding a path to success* (London: Advanced Institute of Management Research, 2006).

with practice and frequently virtually nothing to do with the classroom. This makes many tenured and tenure-track professors feel relieved because they are often mediocre teachers – but it can also make them angry because they realize their own limitations when it comes to practice and to the classroom. Adjuncts can either feel as though they are treated as second-class citizens and/or feel they can do whatever they want. In the former case, they are frustrated; in the latter case, they might become complacent. A venture capitalist evaluating a start-up team would consider such a constellation of separated (and mutually suspicious) labor an "explosive cocktail" and probably would not finance such a venture.

Along this way of reasoning, another interesting report on the future of business schools in the UK came up with the following model for how a business school's activities might be focused (Figure 1.1). The authors then discuss how the following three critical issues – recruitment and retention, dissemination and impact and reputation – might be handled differently, in a tailor-made way, in each of the four settings – professional schools, knowledge economy, liberal arts and social science.

IMD would be considered a "professional school," perhaps with a "knowledge economy" slant. Ivory et al. recommend the following for deans in this respect:

- **Recruitment and retention**: Professional schools need to recruit and retain faculty who are capable of having significant organizational impact through teaching that is well grounded in theory and practice.
- **Dissemination and impact**: Professional schools will maximize their impact through well-designed and delivered teaching and learning programs.
- **Reputation**: The external reputation of professional schools will be heavily influenced by mass media and particularly by program rankings.[28]

NOT ALL BUSINESS SCHOOLS ARE THE SAME

The overall theme of this book is to bring forward general propositions about how to manage business schools more effectively. In doing so, I have used examples from IMD broadly, but let us keep in mind that all business schools are different and there are many ways to effectively manage them. One should be careful not to put unilateral emphasis on one approach. This proviso should be kept closely in mind when reading this book, for I am *not* implying that the IMD way is "the only way!" There are many differentiating factors to consider.

Freestanding or not

Depending on whether a business school is freestanding or not, there are significant implications, particularly with regard to autonomy and speed. There are some freestanding business schools, primarily in

---

[28] Ivory, Miskell, Shipton, White, Moeslein and Neely, *The future of business schools in the UK*, 20.

Europe, e.g. INSEAD, London Business School (which is technically part of the University of London, but *de facto* is freestanding) and IMD. However, the majority of leading business schools are part of a larger university – Harvard Business School, Chicago Graduate School of Business, Stanford Graduate School of Business, Yale School of Management, Northwestern's Kellogg School of Management and the Wharton School of the University of Pennsylvania, to name a few. Creating sufficient "room to maneuver" is key for these schools. Harvard Business School, while technically part of Harvard University, enjoys a considerable degree of autonomy; therefore, it has many of the same benefits as a freestanding business school. At the same time, it benefits from the broader intellectual base of the university. For instance, the Harvard Business School has a joint Ph.D. program with the Department of Economics, as well as with the Departments of Psychology and Sociology.

Size

Leading business schools, such as Harvard or Wharton, each with approximately 225 professors, are clearly large. At the other extreme, we find small schools, such as the Tuck School of Business at Dartmouth or Yale School of Management, with a relatively small number of professors, or IMD with only 55 professors. The benefits of a larger school are many: a greater depth of resources to undertake new research and teaching initiatives; a broader base of knowledge covering many relevant disciplines; new developments in the field might in all likelihood be covered by a school's own faculty. A smaller school, on the other hand, may have less bureaucracy, a less formal administration, simpler decision-making processes and, thus, perhaps the ability to innovate more rapidly. The development of a novel MBA program at Yale, for instance, in a record amount of time, is a good example of such a rapid innovation capability.[29] INSEAD, a

---

[29] D. Bradshaw, "Dean profile: Joel Podolny of Yale," *FT.com*, www.ft.com (January 29, 2007), accessed August 30, 2007.

much larger school than IMD, has a total of eight deans, while IMD has only two. The result is that IMD probably makes quicker decisions and has less fragmentation.

The size of a school will dictate what the most effective options are for management processes and administration. Only with small schools, such as IMD, can a truly "minimalistic" approach to administration be achieved. Larger schools would need more formal processes and structures.

Technological links

Innovations increasingly seem to have a strong technological component. Thus, business schools might benefit by having a close relationship with technological centers of excellence, such as science or engineering schools. The Sloan School of Management, for instance, is working closely with the rest of MIT. Stanford seems to have increasing links with the school of engineering. Some schools will have to look outside for alliances. IMD, for instance, has cooperative agreements with leading technological universities, such as EPFL (in Lausanne), ETH (in Zurich) and MIT/Sloan School (in Cambridge, Massachusetts). Clearly, effective cooperation requires some harmonizing when it comes to cultures and, above all, the development of mutual respect.

Academic conventions

As noted, most universities are built up around conventional academic structures. This is also true for many business schools, particularly when they are part of a university setting. What are the pros and cons of these conventions for managing a business school? Throughout this book, I will delve into the pros and cons for each of the following conventions:

> Tenure: Almost all leading business schools, except IMD, seem to grant tenure to their professors. I know of only one other

business school that has abandoned tenure – Macquarie University's business school in Sydney, Australia.

Academic departments: Clearly, the decision of whether or not to have academic departments is related to size. A larger school would have to resort to academic departments as a way of managing the added complexity that comes with size.

Academic titles: Again, most business schools seem to have academic titles, which are associated with "promoting" faculty and/or renewing their academic contracts. This, too, is perhaps related to size. If a school is small, such as IMD, there may be different ways to assess performance and contract renewal rather than via formal title/hierarchy-related hurdles.

Focused or diverse strategy: Some leading business schools choose a rather diverse set of academic value-creating activities, both nationally and internationally, which tends to lead to more variety in teaching opportunities, i.e. a richer context. The Kellogg School at Northwestern University, for example, seems to thrive on following a relatively large and diverse set of strategic initiatives, that include many types of MBA programs, international relationships, etc. At the other extreme, one can find highly focused schools, with fewer and less conflicting priorities. IMD, for example, is largely focused on executive development programs, although it has a small, but important, high-quality MBA program. IESE in Barcelona perhaps could be seen also as being heavily focused on executive development. Schools that could be classified as being "in between" might include Harvard Business School or INSEAD.

The international dimension: A number of business schools are engaged in academic value-creating activities internationally, often complementing what is being offered at their original campus. INSEAD is one school that has gone far in this direction. It has established teaching campuses in Singapore and Abu Dhabi, with permanent in-residence faculty members.

The University of Chicago has also established teaching activities at several campuses, including Singapore and London. In this case, the faculty members are based in Chicago and travel back and forth for short-term teaching assignments. Intellectual interaction among the members of one group, as opposed to a more fragmented group of faculty, is more easily achieved. Harvard Business School abandoned having a separate faculty residing in Mont-Pèlerin, Switzerland – an experiment it undertook in the 1970s–1980s. It now has six research centers worldwide with only one faculty group based in Cambridge, Massachusetts. By providing local support – i.e. research associates and administrators – the research centers facilitate more effective internationally based research for faculty members who want to undertake research in a particular area, e.g. geography, etc. IESE, in Barcelona, is another example of a school with many strategic alliances, particularly in Latin America, but with fundamentally one faculty group at its home campus. Likewise, IMD has research centers in Shanghai and Mumbai, but its faculty group resides in Lausanne.

Even though a business school may not have an aggressive international strategy, it should be pointed out that a certain degree of fragmentation can still exist. For a variety of reasons – dual careers, schooling of family members, etc. – faculty members are increasingly choosing to live away from the campuses where they work. While this means that the faculty may not be able to work as closely together as one team intellectually, the shortage of qualified faculty members has made this a reality that business schools must accept.

Certainly, many high-performance business schools with different operating models exist. While the examples cited in this book provide insight into IMD's model, the degree to which they can be generalized and used in a particular context must be assessed. Some schools may simply operate in contexts that may make it difficult to follow an approach that works well elsewhere. Business schools have many options to choose from when developing their academic value-creation model. As long as the model is well thought out, is consistent and supported by a committed faculty and administration, good results are possible.

CHANGE IS INEVITABLE

Business schools must accept that, paradoxically, change is probably the only constant upon which they can count. In a world where everything is changing, this is crucial. Looking back, we can perhaps see that the business environment is becoming even more unstable and fluctuating constantly. For example, given the rapid emergence and integration of China and other economies, such as India and Eastern Europe, into the global economy, these emerging economies have become important competitive arenas for businesses. The business community has accepted this and, to some extent, so have many business schools. Businesses have thus come up with new ways of operating in an increasingly boundaryless society and business schools are focusing their research on practical ways to meet these current and emerging challenges occurring in the marketplace. To stay at the cutting edge, the close dialogue between research and teaching – between prescriptive and propositional knowledge – is probably more critical than ever.

One of the basic problems facing many business schools is that they have often been late to grasp what fundamental changes are going on in the business environment. As they have scrambled to try to catch up and stay in step with reality, they have repeatedly found that they lacked the intellectual or financial resources to do so. The intellectual value-creating process has often broken down because of a "disconnect" between prescriptive and propositional knowledge. Professors presented their theories *ex cathedra*. They were often so abstract that even good practitioners could not understand them. And the feedback the practitioners gave to professors often fell on deaf ears.

Following are some of the practical problems and issues that leading business clients now tend to raise. This certainly also creates opportunities – the glass is half-full, not half-empty:

- Learning partner companies increasingly expect to be more involved in the design phase of an executive program, which typically calls for more upfront program development. A challenge for the business school in this situation is to maintain its integrity and professionalism, not letting the learning partner unilaterally dominate the design process.

- Corporations and practicing mangers tend to put a heavy emphasis on how business schools are ranked in leading newspapers such as the *Financial Times* or the *Wall Street Journal*. They view the rankings as an important source in terms of assessing thought leadership. Most business school professors and staff, on the other hand, acknowledge that thought leadership is created primarily through research. While rankings tend to assume that schools are more or less alike, in reality, of course, each school has a different profile and different strengths and weaknesses. To use rankings as an indicator for thought leadership is thus questionable.

- Learning partners increasingly want to know what the expected return is on their executive development investments – how will it affect their bottom line! As a result, more executive programs are being designed with an action-learning component, which could include real-life project-based learning, outdoor leadership exercises, simulations, etc., where the particular actions of the participants will have a consequence.

- More and more often, the executive development decisions for the typical learning partner are driven by human resources specialists and learning officers. In some cases, perhaps for personal career reasons, they tend to be rather risk averse or conservative when it comes to designing programs. This may also be the case when deciding which school to work with. This raises the question as to whether the innovative side of executive education might suffer.

- Learning partners will expect a high degree of flexibility from business schools; for instance, they may want more transparency when it comes to faculty expertise, the ability to choose among various faculty members, access to "cherry pick" faculty for internal projects, further clarity regarding fees for faculty services, etc. Do we run the risk of becoming too unilaterally focused on learning partners' demands, even when these might become quite unreasonable? Is the critical balance between the two sides of the learning partnership being lost?

Some business schools, in an attempt to respond to change, have developed a variety of executive programs to bring insights from research and practical experience together in contexts that are better suited to busy leading executives. With the promise of even stronger take-home insights – based on the interaction of prescriptive and propositional knowledge – it is no wonder that executive education is growing in relative importance in the typical business school's activity portfolio. However, these executive programs vary greatly in the quality of the educational experience that they deliver to executives. Those schools that pay attention to their clients' needs and maintain high-quality classroom activities based on relevant research will survive; those that don't, those that instead offer short, perhaps even entertaining, "dog and pony shows" may fail. There has to be a clear link between the research/thought leadership – the propositional side – and actual practice – the prescriptive side.

Are there economies of scale with regard to research at large business schools? Can we expect a wave of consolidation among business schools so that there will be more concentration within the "business school industry," thereby changing the success parameters for what might be required to be a leading school? Clearly, we would expect some shakeouts in which low-quality business schools might disappear. Beyond this, however, there does not seem to be much in the way of economies of scale for large business schools. In fact, the larger the school, the slower, more rigid and less flexible it may be. Perhaps there is a certain minimum size requirement of, say, fifty to sixty professors and the accompanying capability to avoid bureaucracy and "kingdom building" in developing strong research, strong cutting-edge teaching programs, and strong branding and marketing. Beyond this, however, it is not clear that greater size actually adds to the creation of academic value and strength. Here, I would like to point out that IMD seems to do reasonably well relative to its much larger competitors. Its small size might lead to focus, agility, speed and flexibility. But some small business schools are remarkably unfocused. As we shall see later, leadership is also needed to gain focus. IMD's small size offers the potential for agility, speed and flexibility and it demands focus if the school is to be successful.

How should a business school *adapt* to new opportunities? The answer should be linked probably to a willingness to embrace new segments that offer strong potential for future growth and where academic value can be created. The dilemma for many business schools is that much of their intellectual capability tends to be centered on classical axiomatic research that may have had an obvious place in the past, but that may not necessarily be what is required for a school to embrace the growth opportunities for the future. What may have been a school's strengths in the past may no longer serve it well for the future.

How then can a business school adapt? One answer would be to attempt to develop a relatively clear vision of the emerging segments that might offer reasonable growth opportunities and then to attempt to allow the school's competence base to evolve accordingly in order to take advantage of such emerging opportunities. Figure 1.2 offers such a view: The starting point for IMD would be its commitment to executive programs (Stage I) – in terms of its research capabilities, faculty's abilities to deliver relevant programs, the administrative support and the physical infrastructure. A logical extension might be to embrace executive development (Stage II) which would focus on the lifelong learning needs of individual executives, so that a set of

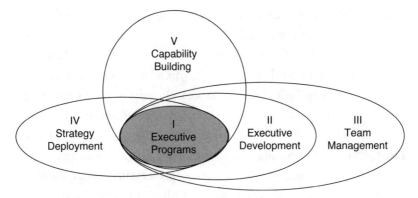

FIGURE 1.2 The potential evolving scope of IMD's activities (and evolving growth strategy).

Source: J.-F. Manzoni, "IMD's business model committee – Presentation to IMD's executive committee," Lausanne, April 5, 2007, p. 12.

programs can be offered over time that would develop execution and other relevant capabilities as the executive evolves into new, typically more all-encompassing, leadership roles. An important aspect of this might be for a school to offer coaching support to executives, to allow for a more effective evolution of their executive development.

Team management (Stage III) is another segment that might offer growth potential. Here the business school might be asked to work with specific corporations re their portfolio of managers – their pool of managerial talent. Models for assessing emerging needs, and thus talent gaps for given firms might then lead to the offering of a planned portfolio of executive development programs. Together with the firm's leadership – typically the top management together with its human resources function – a talent management program can be implemented. Assessments of the talent pool might be important here, using instruments such as Myers-Briggs, the so-called 360° feedback tool and/or through a corporate culture strength/weakness assessment.

Another direction for pursuing future growth might be to focus more on strategy deployment (Stage IV). Action learning, based on the specific strategic dilemmas that a firm faces might be an example of this. At IMD, Peter Killing and Tom Malnight have developed a capability for this – the so-called Must Win Battles approach.[30] Another approach for such strategy development is the so-called deep dive methodology, developed by Andrew Boynton and William Fisher.[31]

Specific capability building (Stage V) might be another segment for growth re academic value-creation. One example of such a capability that might be built is team performance, i.e. "we, we, we" rather than "me, me, me." Boynton and Fisher address this issue. Another example might be to structure implementation capabilities. Xavier Gilbert and Bettina Büchel, with Rhoda Davidson, have developed an approach focused on how to improve the success of implementing strategic initiatives.[32]

Figure 1.2 offers an illustrative picture of how a school such as IMD might evolve. It is clear that the intellectual capability mix of the school must also evolve accordingly – hence, the importance of an explicit human resources management strategy for a school. Without an active HRM approach – to be discussed in Chapter 6 – it is hard to see how a business school's academic value-creation can evolve, except in a random fashion.

IMPLICATIONS FOR BUSINESS SCHOOLS

So what does all this mean for business schools that want to create solid academic value and perhaps be global players in the business of executive education? I have written numerous articles on the subject, some of which, as already mentioned, have been used as the basis for this book (see Appendix II). I have also "seen action" in the classrooms of business schools around the world. In my opinion, there are two factors, above all, that play a critical role in the success of business schools:

[30] J. P. Killing, T. Malnight and T. Keys, *Must-win battles: How to win them, again and again* (Upper Saddle River, NJ: Wharton School Publishing, 2006).
[31] A. Boynton and B. Fisher, *Virtuoso teams: Lessons from teams that changed their worlds* (Harlow: FT Prentice Hall, 2005).
[32] X. Gilbert, B. Büchel and R. Davidson, *Smarter execution* (Harlow: FT Prentice Hall, forthcoming).

1. *Relevant, practitioner-oriented research:* There must be a strong research commitment, which is translated rapidly into teaching and ultimately into thought leadership in teaching! Furthermore, the research needs to be relevant to practitioners; it is no longer enough to wheel out the "old truths." Although academia often looks down on research that is more eclectic, this is often exactly the kind of propositional knowledge that practitioners can understand – and can learn from in the two-way lead and be led process.

2. *Culturally diverse, high-caliber participants:* The increasing role of the practitioner as a key variable in the research equation is relatively new. This calls for a strong focus on relevance, dynamism and change! The competence levels of the class – ideally made up of practicing managers – must be high in order for propositional knowledge and prescriptive knowledge to cross-fertilize each other through a realistic dialogue in the classroom. It is only when there is a global set of high-caliber participants, with different prescriptive knowledge bases, that the value-creating learning process works at its best. We see that there are very few universal prescriptions – most things can be seen very differently, depending on where the participants are from. A culturally diverse group of participants with strong experience is thus key to providing the prescriptive knowledge base in the classroom.

In my view, ultimately any type of business education involves a strong face-to-face component. Webcasts and distance learning – to be discussed later – can be useful complements, but there has to be a face-to-face reunion of participants, at least at the beginning of a learning experience. Also, business education is education for judgment, and as judgment is nuanced, it is thus easier to discuss and teach through physical presence. Body language and quick interactions between professor and learning partners enhance the learning experience considerably. This is why the metaphor of "meeting place" is so important. It involves a high level of face-to-face contact.

IMD in a nutshell

IMD is a self-owned foundation, which is operated on a not-for-profit basis. Although the school is run along similar principles to those found in many other types of healthy businesses, the net financial proceeds are reinvested in faculty (salaries, research support, etc.), staff, buildings and the like. No dividends are paid to any outside owners; no "taxes" are paid to a university. The school has no debt and receives no financial support from any federal, cantonal or communal governments. IMD is entirely on its own and responsible for its own success. The annual turnover is approximately CHF113 million, or US$83.5 million. There are 55 full-time professors at IMD and a support staff of approximately 250.

IMD is very international – perhaps even the most international of the world's leading business schools. This applies to both IMD people and participants – there are currently about twenty-eight different nationalities represented in the faculty. Our international mix of participants comes from Europe, including the former Eastern Europe (51 per cent); the Americas (19 per cent), of which about half are from the US and Canada; and Asia (26 per cent) of which about 6 per cent are from Japan and 7 per cent from the Middle East (primarily the Gulf area and Saudi Arabia). China is still a relatively small market for IMD, but the fastest growing one.

Of course, there have been challenges – even problems – along the way. The faculty are absolutely central to achieving success for a business school – they must be top quality. For IMD, with its unique model for academic value-creation, this has resulted in some particular challenges:

1. *Faculty recruiting:* To attract the best faculty members is a challenge for all business schools. At IMD, we are looking for both excellence in research, but with managerial relevance (not necessarily in the more conventional axiomatic sense)

and strong pedagogical abilities (again with a focus on managerial relevance). And the faculty must be comfortable in a two-way interactive learning environment. In order to have the desired competence profile, faculty members will typically have several years of teaching experience before joining IMD. But, why would they want to leave the business school they are currently at, particularly if they are successful? In practice, many faculty members leave a school when they are not granted tenure. However, as we discuss in the book, the decision-making process leading to tenure is often rather random and based on traditional axiomatic measures. Hence, excellent faculty members who perhaps may not meet the requirements for tenure at their current axiomatically focused schools, may still have an excellent profile in terms of the eclecticism that IMD is looking for. By recruiting faculty who are outstanding when it comes to managerially relevant research and teaching, IMD avoids the image of hiring "rejects."

Why not hire young faculty members directly out of Ph.D. programs? It turns out that it can be difficult for them to integrate effectively at IMD – their lack of managerially relevant teaching and/or research experience can represent a real barrier! At IMD, our track record for hiring and developing young faculty members fresh out of Ph.D. programs has not been good.

2. *Closeness to customers:* Much of the development of new teaching programs *vis-à-vis* corporate clients takes place through IMD's corporate development directors (CDDs) or field force. The CDDs typically have an MBA degree or equivalent and several years of experience, preferably in the business-to-business marketing area. They negotiate the commercial terms, delivery schedules, etc. with clients. The faculty are deliberately kept out of this process for the most part. On occasion, of course, a faculty member may be called

on to "help" land a particular assignment. Most of the time, however, the faculty will step in at the program design stage and, thereafter, during the actual delivery of the program. While this process generally works well, it also has some weaknesses. Perhaps the biggest weakness has to do with managing the clients' expectations in terms of faculty involvement during the early marketing phase of the process. At the risk of disappointing the learning partner, we have decided to preserve faculty capacity for academic design and delivery rather than have them involved in the entire process. In the end, however, IMD's faculty deliver outstanding programs and our learning partners tend to be more than satisfied with the result.

3. *Conflict with private consulting:* Faculty members at IMD do have the opportunity to do private consulting, in line with what would be the norm at all leading business schools. The faculty guidelines indicate that up to 45 days of a faculty member's time might be spent on this per year. It is further stated that this cannot be undertaken if it conflicts with IMD. Thus, for instance, a team of faculty members could not offer an executive development program that naturally would "belong" to IMD. At times it might be difficult to distinguish between "what is IMD's business" and "what is private business." For instance, faculty members might be tempted by attempts from certain companies to "cherry pick" faculty for, say, a one-day session in their corporate university. While this may not be an issue initially, it could become one if an in-depth relationship develops between the individual faculty member and a company. At IMD, each faculty member reports on his/her outside work activities to help regulate these potential conflicts.

4. *The ageing of the faculty team:* It is typically preferred that faculty members at IMD arrive with a fair amount of work

experience – from academia and/or from practice – after
having completed their formal doctoral training. Thus, most
IMD professors have about ten years of teaching experience
or more behind them before being hired by IMD. It is a real
problem to find qualified and experienced professors, who
are comfortable with IMD's type of academic value-creation
and who feel uncomfortable enough with the classic models
for creating academic value found in most business schools
to want to make the switch. Because of the difficulty we face
in recruiting enough qualified faculty, it has become a challenge to keep the average age of the faculty stable, and not
rising!

2   Key academic programs and academic value-creation

> To fuel imagination and innovation, learning must be continuous and applied creatively and rapidly. New ways of thinking, diverse perspectives, leadership courage and smart execution will characterize the next generation of successful organizations. In order to win, tomorrow's successful executives will have to combine insight with the art and science of management.
>
> Paul Strebel and Tracey Keys[1]

KEY POINTS

- Increasingly, the bulk of a business school's academic programs will be aimed at leading executives who are also learning partners.
- However, an elite MBA program will also be a significant factor, as it ensures that there is proper in-depth treatment of new knowledge, over a sufficient number of classes, to guarantee academic value-creation.[2] MBAs are also important learning partners!
- Open-enrollment executive programs ensure breadth of participation by executives from many leading companies and countries. The learning effect of the "global meeting place" can be significant.
- Tailored, in-company programs ensure in-depth treatment of a specific company's strategic issues, often via "action learning," to come up with implementable results.
- Open-enrollment executive programs and in-company programs complement each other; both offer unique sources of learning, and leading companies-cum-learning partners would make use of both.

---

[1] P. Strebel and T. Keys (eds.), *Mastering executive education: How to combine content with context and emotion – The IMD guide* (Harlow: FT Prentice Hall/ Pearson Education, 2005).

[2] Please note that the MBA program and the Executive MBA program represent different paths toward earning the same degree at IMD – the MBA degree. When we refer to the MBA program, we are including the Executive MBA program, unless stated otherwise.

- Both types of programs complement each other financially too. Open-enrollment programs have a high upside financial potential, when the class is full! In-company programs are offered for a fixed fee – more financial stability, but less financial upside.
- Other offerings such as coaching and effective learning networks can add to a school's value-creation by broadening the circle for obtaining valuable insights. Such activities can also leverage – and thus free up – some faculty time, thereby paving the way for even more research!

INTRODUCTION

In a rapidly changing global business environment, with increasingly blurred boundaries, knowledge is becoming recognized as a competitive advantage. Organizations want executive education that does more than inform. They want business schools to link their theories to practice to push change quickly through the organization, ultimately to improve the bottom line. As Arie de Geus put it, "The ability to learn faster than your competitors may be the only sustainable competitive advantage."[3] And as the landscape continues to broaden, companies want business schools to develop not only leaders but also *global* leaders. Action learning, thought leadership, globalization, cross-cultural aptness, leading in flat organizations and the like are increasingly becoming requirements.

How can business schools address the demands of their learning partners to deliver programs that are truly leading edge, practical and global in content? At IMD, we see it in terms of a virtuous cycle of value-creation between research and our key academic programs – the MBA programs (including the Executive MBA), executive programs (both open enrollment and in-company) and IMD's Learning Network all provide IMD's faculty with the opportunity to collaborate actively with companies and practicing managers for their research and

[3] A. de Geus, "Planning as learning," *Harvard Business Review* 66 (1988), 70.

FIGURE 2.1 Virtuous cycle of value-creation.

teaching. The essence of this value-creation – for both academia and business practice – as we have already mentioned, is based on a lead and be led premise, on "running both in front of the cart and behind it." Cutting-edge research, in the form of thought leadership-type propositions, is brought to participants in the classroom while it is still fresh – and these participants are hopefully leading executives from all over the world. They can add further inputs to the research propositions, typically seeing them in the context of prescriptive, experience-based dilemmas. Projects, actually project-based action research – undertaken by faculty as well as participants on real-life issues – can be particularly effective here. Hence, practice not only learns from academia, but also leads academia; it is an interactive process for adding insight – propositional knowledge meets prescriptive knowledge!

In Figure 2.1, we can see how each set of key academic programs might feed into the others and also the two-way interface between research and the classroom. And, significantly, we see that there is *a single* faculty group driving all of this – not separate sub-faculties for research, the MBA programs, executive education and so on.

The MBA programs represent a vital opportunity when it comes to research entering the classroom. This reflects the fact that the dialogue between the faculty and the participants *cum* learning partners will typically go on for more classroom sessions, in contrast to the fewer sessions typically offered in shorter executive programs. Hence, there is the potential for more in-depth exchange and value enhancement – particularly if the MBA class is of the highest caliber, truly international with considerable managerial experience. And the faculty will have more time to refine and accelerate the development of new knowledge.

Open executive programs are another likely source of interaction between research and practice in the classroom. During these programs, there is clearly also a "global meeting place" effect, with the participation of able executives from a variety of companies around the world. Tailored in-company programs perhaps offer somewhat less potential for this type of joint learning because the participants all come from one company, although as they may come from all over the world, there are still often good opportunities for academic value-creation.

IMD's Learning Network (discussed in detail later in this chapter) provides opportunities for faculty to collaborate with leading companies and executives so that their research agendas are relevant and at the forefront of current and emerging business issues. Research/ practitioner dialogue can take place in many areas and provide a multitude of opportunities for value-creation.

At IMD, we strive to keep a balance between our open-enrollment programs and our in-company programs – for both academic value-creation reasons and commercial reasons. Academically, it is key for "learning in the breadth" (open-enrollment programs) *and* "learning in the depth" (tailored programs). Clearly the two complement each other! Commercially, the open-enrollment programs can be compared with scheduled airline routes; there is a high commercial yield if the programs are filled up – high load factors! The tailored programs, by contrast, can be compared with the chartered airline business – steady, but with less upside; you sell a program, or make the plane available, and that is it!

The executive programs generate a significant proportion of the funds that provide the economic base for leading business schools, such as IMD, to recruit the best faculty and invest in research, teaching materials and facilities. This, in turn, benefits all programs, including the MBA degree programs, which, as we have seen, can play a unique and positive role when it comes to academic value-creation. However, from an economic standpoint, the full-time MBA program tends to be relatively less critical as a positive financial contributor to a business school's economic base – in many business schools, the MBA program is even a loss leader. At IMD, however, the Executive MBA program is a significant financial contributor to the school's economic base.

In this chapter, we will elaborate on how diversity, interaction in the classroom and faculty collaboration with business can contribute to creating maximum value for a business school's learning partners. And of course, in the two-way learning process, the faculty and their research benefit too.

Also, new organizations are entering the executive education arena intensifying and broadening competition – traditional business schools are no longer the sole players. In this chapter, we shall also briefly review these new entrants.

OPEN-ENROLLMENT PROGRAMS

changing the rules, or suspending them, could be a spur to learning. Rules in a corporation are extremely important. Nobody likes them but everybody obeys them because they are recognized as the glue of the organization. And yet, we have all known extraordinary managers who got their organizations out of a rut by changing the rules. Intuitively, they changed the organization and the way it looked at matters, and so, as a consequence, accelerated learning.[4]

[4] De Geus, "Planning as learning," 70.

And as Charles Darwin is quoted as saying in his *On the Origin of Species*, "It is not the strongest of the species that survives, nor the most intelligent that survives. It is the one that is the most adaptable to change." The above quotes underscore the most significant challenge facing companies and business schools today – how do they keep up with the pace and scale of knowledge-generation and change in the world?

The answer probably lies in developing a stronger adaptive capacity and a more genuine will within the organization to be responsive to change. If they are to survive, organizations must encourage ongoing renewal. Business schools can significantly assist in this, particularly with open-enrollment executive programs. Executives who participate in these programs will learn not only from the faculty but also from a broad cross-section of leading executives. They will discover new ways to think and behave so that they are better equipped to introduce the business reforms that will improve the effectiveness of their companies.

For maximum impact, open-enrollment programs should attract executives from a diverse array of companies, industries and cultures to gather in the "global meeting place" – ideal for the lead and be led type of academic value-creation described in Chapter 1. A central challenge for management educators is to design a multifaceted, comprehensive approach to global business education while encompassing the different cultural perspectives of the students. Thought leadership, being the result of the faculty's heavy focus on research – albeit of a practical nature – will thus be a particularly important part of this. Business schools must thus typically offer executive programs that capture the key issues of globalization, in terms of the context in which the class is given. These are usually dilemmas – without simple answers. Examples of contextual dilemmas could include long-term versus short-term performance goals; top-line versus bottom-line focus; teams versus individuals; hierarchical versus flat organizational structures; and authoritative decision-making versus broad, participative decision-making.

In open-enrollment programs, perhaps more than in any other type of executive program, except possibly the MBA, the professor drives the learning agenda by bringing conceptual thinking (the propositional knowledge described by Mokyr[5]) into the classroom. Some of these insights and theories will be empirically based case studies or other types of small-scale field research, while others may be conceptual. As noted, the context of most of this research would be international in scope, meet the cross-disciplinary demands of real business situations and be at the forefront of current and evolving business issues. It must reflect reality!

The intention, of course, is to provoke strong reactions, insights and suggestions from the participants so that they further improve the research by offering their prescriptive knowledge, i.e. their practical experiences of approaches that have or have not worked for them. This interaction and continuous feedback between the professor and the participants is critical, as it sets the stage for everyone to gain new knowledge and deeper insights on an ongoing basis and, above all, it avoids the dry delivery of abstract theories by the professor. Hence, a gradual evolution in both theory and practice unfolds. And when the process is well executed, it often results in those cherished "Aha!" moments – those moments when you gain insights that go far beyond straightforward problem solving.[6]

Let me provide an illustration. During IMD's Building High Performance Boards program, I gave a session on "the dos and don'ts" when it comes to being an effective board member. My research findings were based on clinical work and propositional insights gained by examining the workings of several boards. The reactions to these conceptual propositions were manifold:

- A Swiss executive felt that by bringing all of these items up, one would totally overwhelm management and bring the work of the board to a standstill. He prescribed a much simpler approach!

---

[5] J. Mokyr, *The gifts of Athena* (Princeton, NJ: Princeton University Press, 2002).
[6] Strebel and Keys (eds.), *Mastering executive education.*

- A US-based executive felt that documentation of corporate practices, as they relate to each of these items, would be a key aspect of safeguarding oneself against litigation. He prescribed more detailed, written documentation.
- A Europe-based member felt that the implied questioning of the authority of senior management might raise problems. He prescribed strong leadership at the top – not to be challenged!

All of the above comments are "correct," but neither they, nor my initial propositions, captured the whole truth. But, taken together, a richer, more meaningful picture of what constitutes effective working behavior at the board level materialized. As a result, we obtained an enriched, multifaceted picture.

> ## IMD's open-enrollment programs
> With more than twenty programs, IMD offers one of the world's most comprehensive ranges of open-enrollment executive education. The programs vary in length from several days to ten weeks, and they are designed to address the real needs of practicing managers around the world and at various stages of their careers.
>
> IMD's aim is that each program should reflect recent original research, provide true thought leadership and draw heavily on original learning materials, ideally developed at IMD. These materials must of course be stimulating and challenging, emphasizing the development of leadership skills and new competencies in the context of true value-creation within the "global meeting place," where deeper insights result from this enlightened classroom interaction.
>
> Perhaps one particularly good example of this faculty–participant value-creation is IMD's Orchestrating Winning Performance program (OWP). All of IMD's professors – 55 in total – participate in this six-day program. And virtually all of the material that they present is new, based on their most

recent research. An amazingly strong group of more than 540 global executives, representing 57 countries, with a total of almost 12,000 years of experience, work actively with the propositions put forward by the faculty.[7] Partly, this is done through networking in large plenary sessions, but most of the classroom sessions (many of which are run in parallel) provide a smaller forum for networking with groups of 40 to 50 executives. The result is exceptional, mind-expanding learning for most of the participants and enhanced research insights for the faculty, as reflected by the many original cases and articles coming out of the OWP process.

Why do so many executives want to attend this program? The main reason is probably that the market has recognized the unique learning opportunity at hand – with virtually all new research-based materials and great networking. It is a true example of the lead and be led principle!

At IMD, we are finding that the open-enrollment program portfolio needs to be actively managed. Specifically, new programs must be well researched, in terms of assessing the market potential. And the faculty must inject thought leadership into the programs so that they are indeed cutting edge. Two recently introduced programs did indeed have these characteristics – "Low Cost Competition" and "Take Risks, Get Growth!"

Still, it typically takes a relatively long time for a new program to "get up to speed." Word-of-mouth seems to be particularly important, and companies typically want to try out a program before they commit to sending more executives. Thus, the introduction of a new program into the portfolio is clearly drawn out – it takes longer than one would expect!

As for established programs, they need constant renewal in order to stay successful. New features, stemming from recent

---

[7] IMD's Orchestrating Winning Performance Program, 2006 figures.

research, must be introduced into the programs. Brochures and websites must be updated with these new features articulated. The program directors for open-enrollment programs must also "rotate" on a regular basis, say, every third or fourth year. A new program director will tend to look at a program with fresh eyes, which will result in innovation and perhaps more energy in the marketplace.

While the overall portfolio of IMD's open-enrollment programs is constantly evolving, it is nevertheless constrained by the availability of new program directors, the flow of new ideas coming from research and the relatively long introduction time typically required for new programs. Inputs from the marketplace are thus not driving the open program portfolio alone. Rather, it is the combination of marketplace inputs and internal competencies that tend to shape the portfolio.

IN-COMPANY PROGRAMS

Company-specific programs must be developed according to the individual client's particular strategic needs and learning objectives. In order to achieve this, the development process requires close partnership and ongoing dialogue at all levels of the organization, with a view to identifying the appropriate scope, style and orchestration of the final program.[8]

In contrast to open-enrollment programs, in-company programs bring groups of executives from the same company together to build shared in-depth competencies, implement coordinated change more rapidly, develop or renew strategies and/or prepare execution plans for implementation. Back at the office, the executives then act on what they

---

[8] S. Meehan, "Company-specific program design: Supporting the roll out of a new corporate strategy," in Strebel and Keys (eds.), *Mastering executive education*.

have worked on at IMD and put it into practice. This action-learning component is typically an integral part of the design of these programs, and for the company it is often a way to accelerate the rollout of a new strategy.

Developing this type of high-impact learning experience requires that both the company and the business school contribute their best to the program creation process. The company brings a deep understanding of its organization and its culture, and its experience will drive the prescriptive part of the learning agenda. The business school brings the propositional thought leadership through its research and its experience in program design and delivery. The faculty team introduces relevant, propositional insights stemming from their own research. As always, these insights are presented in a way that is meaningful for the participants and tailored to the specific requirements of the company. In doing so, the faculty will hopefully inspire the team of executives with challenging new ideas and alternatives that the executives, in turn, and as a result of their prescriptive insights, can apply to the issues facing the company. Thus, by applying the concepts introduced by the faculty to the real issues the executives are dealing with, the learning through interaction is enhanced for participants and faculty alike.

In order for this to work, both partners must trust, challenge and encourage each other and share a common commitment to strive for the success of the learning process. Again, the research component is critical when it comes to creating value for in-company learning partners. Equally important is the fact that the participants, despite being from the same company, typically represent an eclectic base – often coming from different countries, a variety of backgrounds, with diverse skills and experience. With this basis for interactive value-creation, the faculty and participants can share and further develop their perspectives and frameworks during the program. In some cases, the company might send intact business unit teams, which can lead to rapid implementation of strategies and action plans, when they return to the business. Furthermore, the learning that comes from this process can be translated into strategies and action plans in the organization. The learning and the business objectives of the company will be driven to new heights – and so will the insights of the faculty!

Often a key challenge is finding a realistic balance between the concepts introduced by the faculty team and the experience base of the organization and the participants. But what happens, for instance, if the participants come primarily from one country, and, on top of this, happen to have more or less the same background, say engineering? The lead and be led, faculty–participant, joint discovery process is less likely to work in this case as there may not be enough variety to create a "global meeting place." How, then, can business schools achieve this high-impact learning ambition? Above all, it will be important for the professors to get out of the classroom, to meet with as great a diversity of people in the company as possible, including those not attending the program, such as the participants' bosses and other colleagues. This should help them to understand, at least to some degree, the unique strategic challenges the company is facing and the cultural context of the organization. The prior preparation by the professors going inside the company will be key. Without this type of collaboration, it is hard to see how cutting-edge executive development can realistically take place.

NEW ACTORS

In addition to traditional business schools, there is, of course, increasingly more competition from other providers of executive education. Consulting firms, for instance, seem to have become more and more focused on executive development. With the emergence of more of an action orientation, it would appear that business schools have become closer to what is normally associated with consulting firms. And the boundaries that define consulting firms and modern business schools with an executive development orientation are likely to become increasingly blurred in the future.

Corporate universities also represent an additional source of competition for business schools. With corporations typically wanting more influence in the development of their own corporate cultures, corporate universities may become a more prominent source for these types of programs in the future.

"Cherry-picking" also represents a source of competition. Several new institutions have grown up drawing on the teaching resources of individual faculty members from various business schools. Duke Corporate Education (Duke CE) and Business Center Europe are successful examples of this. According to the *Financial Times*,

> One of the most controversial aspects of Duke CE is its use of business school professors selected from the world's top institutions. Many of these schools have banned their faculty from working with Duke; they say there is no other industry that would allow its employees to work for a competitor. Duke's response is that if the work is exciting and challenging enough, then the faculty member will take that back to the employer and the business school will benefit. Moreover, the flexibility will enable business schools to retain their star players. It is an argument that has yet to be won.[9]

It is ironic that a business school might end up competing with some of its own faculty members qua individual operators, when one considers that the research, upon which they base themselves, has typically been financed by their business school! When individual faculty members are hired by such institutions based on knowledge they already have, these competitors are able to provide cost-efficient programs, since they do not have to pay for the cost of research to develop and maintain core competencies. Consequently, many business schools have put regulations in place that try to safeguard against this

---

[9] D. Bradshaw, "Tough Act to follow for new Duke CE chief," *Financial Times* (May 14, 2007).

type of competition from their own faculty. These guidelines seem to work well at IMD.

IMD's partnership programs

Partnership programs, also known as in-company programs, are a significant part of IMD's portfolio of activities, representing 41 per cent of the school's revenues (compared with 39 per cent from open-enrollment programs). Each year our faculty design, develop and deliver carefully tailored learning experiences to address the specific learning objectives of our partner companies. These customized programs can help the companies build new capabilities and address their most significant business challenges. But, as noted, it works best when the participant groups are eclectic. And, as also noted, relevant research must be brought to the table – if not, the process will probably not work.

Therefore, when IMD works with companies to develop learning experiences, we build the programs based on each client's unique strategy, culture, business challenges and learning needs. Our faculty members spend a lot of time getting to know our learning partners. The more we know about them and the deeper our relationships are, the more we will be able to bring research issues and conceptual insights that the participants will find relevant and stimulating.

Action learning – an integral part of in-company programs – is increasingly a key component of IMD's academic value-creation. It blends academic expertise and relevant research with hands-on discussions among a strong group of participants from a given company, who then return to work with prepared execution plans. The result, when it works, is accelerated, action-oriented learning, enhanced strategies that are shared broadly within the firm, and faster implementation.

MBA DEGREE PROGRAMS

> No one can create a manager in a classroom. But existing managers can significantly improve their practice in a thoughtful classroom that makes use of that experience.[10]

> Bain [the management consulting firm] believes diversity breeds creativity and we're thus committed to seeking the best talent available to solve complex business problems and industry issues. Different points of view give us more insight into our clients' businesses . . . We also recruit individuals with extensive industry experience. But at the end of the day, an MBA provides a great foundation for success at Bain. MBAs provide the strong generalist background and business fundamentals that our consultants need to implement strategies across industries and yield the best results for our clients.[11]

While there has been steady, and sometimes rapid, growth globally in MBA programs over the last several decades, full-time MBA program applications seemed to reach their peak in 2002. For instance, the number of candidates taking the so-called Graduate Management Admission Test (GMAT) – a prerequisite for entering most MBA programs – fell by 7 per cent in 2003 and 9 per cent in 2004. The demand for MBA programs seems to have bottomed out in 2004.[12] According to the Graduate Management Admission Council (GMAC), "A broad majority of full-time, part-time and executive MBA programs recorded increased application volume [in 2006] compared with the levels they posted a year earlier."[13] The demand for

---

[10] H. Mintzberg, *Managers not MBAs* (Harlow: FT Prentice Hall/Pearson Education, 2004).

[11] Bill Neuenfeldt, Partner and Head of Global Schools Recruiting, Bain & Company, as quoted in "Ask the experts: MBA," *Financial Times* (January 26, 2007).

[12] *Executive summary of key findings: 2005 application trends summary* (McLean, VA: Graduate Management Admission Council, 2005), www.gmac.com, accessed June 9, 2007.

[13] "Business school applications jump across the board in 2006" (McLean, VA: Graduate Management Admission Council, News Release, August 7, 2006), www.gmac.com, accessed June 9, 2007.

MBA programs perhaps has a rather uncertain future. So why should business schools want to tap into this relatively low-growth market? Because, as described earlier, the MBA programs remain a vital part of a business school's portfolio as there can be a strong symbiotic relationship between MBA programs and research-based thought leadership in terms of creating academic value for faculty and students alike.

While many of the world's leading business schools have very large MBA programs, a small MBA program can better accelerate real value-creation at a business school. A smaller program can also ensure top quality through tough admission standards but, above all, it allows for rapid innovations by having only one class – one section – thus avoiding the slow, often endless coordination among multiple sections of larger MBA programs.

To create strong academic value, business schools also need to strive to compete for MBA applicants from the worldwide talent pool. Clearly, however, most business schools will only be able to cater to their local or regional markets. They will not have the necessary global brand recognition, the breadth and quality of faculty or the financial resources to compete in the global top league. These schools – particularly if the program is large and the admission standards are low – will be unlikely to be able to create cutting-edge, fresh academic value that will be enhanced through classroom interactions. Professors will often "give lectures" from materials they have had in the filing cabinet for years, without being exposed to the lead and be led challenge from a diverse group of the brightest students.

According to Mintzberg, the call should be to develop "managers not MBAs."[14] But how? The challenge, it seems, is to bring relevant research-based thought leadership into the curriculum in terms of what students *cum* learning partners will need when they enter the global economy – and in terms of what they can relate to and react to

---

[14] Mintzberg, *Managers not MBAs*.

in a meaningful way. The focus, perhaps, will increasingly be on integrated eclectic offerings from various disciplinary fields. This will be achieved through integrated modular programs, rather than offering semester-long courses in a particular functional, axiomatic area, such as finance, marketing or accounting. Experienced faculty, who are capable of bringing forward relevant and eclectic research insights, will be even more essential.

There is also great value in having faculty who are capable of teaching across the entire portfolio of programs – not just in the MBA program. Many business schools struggle with this. They often hire relatively less experienced, younger faculty members to teach in the MBA program, while more experienced professors teach in the executive programs. The result is a discontinuity of faculty knowledge build-up, so the particularly positive effect of working with the MBAs, as discussed earlier, will not lead to the intended thought leadership benefits in the executive programs.

As with open programs, the point of departure in MBA programs is propositional knowledge – new business concepts based on cross-disciplinary research – which the professor develops further in the MBA classroom by engaging and interacting with the participants. High-quality MBAs, with strong intellectual capabilities and relevant managerial prescriptive insights, often have the time and interest to challenge new concepts being proposed by a faculty member. Thus, when these propositional business concepts are juxtaposed with the prescriptive insights from the participants, the concepts are refined and often lead to new insights – both in terms of research and managerial relevance – a virtuous cycle of academic value-creation.

IMD's MBA degree programs

IMD's MBA programs (full time and Executive MBA) combine innovation, relevance to business, and a unique blend of intensity and dedication to the individual participants. The programs are grounded in the extensive relationships IMD has built over the years with successful global organizations. The emphasis is on developing global leadership capabilities, as well as on enhancing entrepreneurship and business development capabilities.

Each year we limit our full-time MBA program to ninety participants and our Executive MBA program typically has seventy participants. Above all, we keep the programs small because the one-section structure ensures fast innovation. New concepts can be rapidly introduced. Coordination across sections is eliminated.

Also, a small size makes it easier to attract only top quality candidates – above all by eliminating the problem of rapidly decreasing quality at the bottom end of a large class. Our candidates are carefully selected to make up a truly diverse class with complementary skills, nationalities and cultural backgrounds – a group of people who are driven by the desire to make a difference. They are a talented and motivated group of managers (with an average age of 30 and seven years' work experience) who are hungry to learn and eager to share their knowledge and insights. Because of the small size, the hurdle for entry – in terms of both academic achievement and experience – is high. Each candidate is interviewed at IMD. Each year more than 300 admission interviews are conducted – an expensive, but necessary process that shows IMD's commitment to quality.

The Executive MBA program is based on candidates first completing IMD's 2 x 5-week open-enrollment Program for Executive Development (PED). This means that they will be well known to IMD's faculty when they apply to the EMBA program, making the selection process that much easier. Academically, all EMBA candidates must also achieve a reasonable score on the GMAT test, which, of course, is also the case with MBA applicants.

The professors who teach on IMD's MBA degree programs are the same experienced professors who teach on the school's executive programs. As part of IMD's commitment to being a

highly international business school, the faculty members represent about twenty-eight nationalities. They stay abreast of the
changing business environment through a combination of field-
based research, dialoguing with top executives in international
companies and their work in IMD's executive programs. It is
one faculty, one academic team.

IMD'S LEARNING NETWORK

We look to partner with a business school that is prepared to
listen to our point of view and design the program together with
us. A willingness to learn from each other is also very important.
We want our partners to bring business knowledge to the table
and not just academic knowledge.[15]

As we have argued, a strong MBA program should be clearly linked
with good, current business practices. IMD's Learning Network has
been established for this purpose. However, the benefits of this strong
link with leading businesses reach far beyond the MBA program – they
extend to all of IMD's program and research activities. The IMD
Learning Network offers a range of learning opportunities for the managers in its partner companies and provides a platform from which
IMD can strengthen its links with business and deepen its relationships with key learning partners. It is another way for faculty to bring
their thought leadership forward and for business to interact and react,
with tangible benefits on both sides. It is another manifestation of lead
and be led, but in a different context.

More than 175 companies from all over the world participate in
the Learning Network, and the membership list is growing fast.
Through the network, IMD and the participating companies strive to

---

[15] Julie Harrison, responsible for leadership development training, Allianz Management
Institute, a member of the IMD Learning Network, as quoted in B. Büchel and D.
Antunes, "Reflections on executive education: The users' and providers' perspec-
tives," *Academy of Management Learning and Education* 6 (September 2007).

achieve strong, sustainable and mutually beneficial learning partnerships. Each participating company pays an annual fee to become a member. In return, they can benefit, at no additional cost, from a range of learning activities that include:

- *Wednesday Webcasts:* These webcasts feature, for the most part, IMD faculty presenting practical applications of their latest research. Often this research stems from collaboration with the Learning Network companies themselves. Guest CEOs and other top executives are also featured from time to time. These interactive internet broadcasts last approximately 30 minutes and include a live question-and-answer period. A professional interviewer asks the speaker about his or her research results to ensure a practical managerial focus. Presently, about 30,000 executives subscribe to the Wednesday Webcasts with a viewership of up to 3,000 per week, many of whom watch and discuss the transmission in teams. This is likely to add additional benefits for them and their company when it comes to learning. The many participants from business practice can thus continue to learn while on the job, exploring new knowledge frontiers without actually taking time away from work. For the professors, the webcasts offer an opportunity to articulate some propositional state-of-the-art thought based on their current research. It provides a fast way to bring out new ideas, with much more rapid dissemination than through conventional academic publishing channels.
- *IMD podcasts:* Companies increasingly may want their executives to be able to use moments of spare time for reinforcing their learning. This means that there is an increasing demand for presenting thought leadership through new media, such as via the iPod. Executives might thus now listen to and see the professor delivering short new thought leadership messages this way. At IMD, these are developed as condensed versions of the Wednesday Webcasts. The net effect is that the dissemination of new thoughts now becomes even more intense, going on a more continuing basis,

virtually delivered to individual executives wherever they are, even when they are driving to work in their own cars!

- *Discovery events:* Some ten discovery events take place each year at IMD for Learning Network member companies. During these events, professors present and discuss their recent research with executives from member companies. Sometimes, executives also make relevant presentations based on their companies' experiences. The participating executives give valuable feedback and the result is cutting-edge, two-way learning. Everyone learns from everyone else – the professors from the executives and the executives from the professors and from each other. Top executives from member companies bring forward and discuss ways to handle difficult and complex challenges that their companies are facing. These challenges are often instrumental in further shaping the research agenda of the faculty. Propositional knowledge meets prescriptive knowledge.

- *Global Business Forums:* About thirty to forty Global Business Forums – somewhat shorter in length than Discovery Events – take place worldwide each year, featuring IMD faculty. While the primary function of these forums is for marketing purposes, they definitely also represent an important avenue for two-way learning as they bring executives from various parts of the world and IMD's faculty closer together. Fresh research is often presented in these local contexts, frequently resulting in in-depth understanding for all who participate.

- *Communication updates:* Various newsletters, research updates and the like are regularly made available to member companies. One of the most important is the regular publication *Perspectives for Managers*, in which IMD's faculty members present recent research topics in a practical and concise way. The challenge for them is to be minimalist, i.e. to record the practical essence of the research in relatively few words.

- *Business Advisory Council:* Senior human resource managers of all the member companies can participate in the Business

Advisory Council. Key strategic human resources management issues are discussed; for example, recent topics have included "Talent in Its Prime and Talent at Its Peak" and "Work Life Balance." The relevance of the content of IMD's program offerings for the Learning Network companies is also reviewed on an ongoing basis.

- *CEO roundtable:* This annual roundtable is a forum at which senior executives and IMD faculty meet to debate topics that are top of mind for CEOs, such as top management dilemmas, change management, leadership issues, performance measurement, mergers and acquisitions, and the like. Some recent topics have included "Fueling Growth and Strategic Renewal: The CEO's Role," and "China: HR Differentiation as Competitive Advantage." When well scripted, these short events (normally lasting less than a day) can offer considerable value for senior executives. As well as providing new insights into the challenges CEOs are facing, the roundtables also provide an opportunity to build networking relationships with their peers. For the business school, the value is also in building relationships: And the active involvement with senior executives contributes to a deeper understanding of the key dilemmas they face. This understanding can then be used to enrich teaching and focus thought leadership to ensure that IMD continues to offer relevant management development based on the needs of its participants.

EXECUTIVE COACHING

Helping people change is not an easy process. Anybody who tells you a different story, I view as a snake oil salesman. But change is possible as I have seen the remarkable results of the interventions that take place. . .[16]

[16] The Raoul de Vitry d'Avaucourt Professor in Human Resource Management, INSEAD, in "An interview with Manfred Kets de Vries," *Strategic Direction* 23 (2007), 29–31.

Table 2.1 *IMD's corporate learning network – member companies*

Partners

A.P. Møller Maersk	HSBC Holdings plc
ABB Asea Brown Boveri Ltd.	IBM Europe
ABN Amro Bank nv	KONE
Ayala Group	Kuwait Petroleum Corporation
Boston Consulting Group	Mars
BT Group	Nestlé SA
Caterpillar Inc.	Nokia Corporation
Citigroup	Novartis
Credit Suisse Group	PricewaterhouseCoopers
DaimlerChrysler AG	Procter & Gamble AG
Deloitte	Royal Dutch Shell plc
Dentsu Inc.	Royal Philips Electronics
DSM nv	SAP
Du Pont de Nemours International	Swiss Reinsurance Company
Dubai International Financial	Tetra Pak International SA
Centre	The Royal Bank of Scotland plc
F. Hoffmann-La Roche Ltd.	UBS AG
Heerema Holding	Unilever NV
Holcim Ltd.	Zürich Financial Services

Associates

Accenture	Alfa S.A.B. de C.V.
Adecco SA	Allianz AG
ADMA-OPCO	Asahi Glass Co. Ltd.
Aegon The Netherlands nv	ASML Netherlands BV
Air France–KLM	ASSA ABLOY AB
AISTS – International Academy	AXA
of Sports Science and	Ballarpur Industries Ltd.
Technology	Banco Itau SA
Ajinomoto Inc.	Bank Julius Baer
Aker Kvaerner ASA	Barclays Global Investors

Table 2.1 (*cont.*)

BBVA Banco Bilbao Vizcaya Argentaria	Dubai Holding LLC
Bekaert Group	E.ON Academy GmbH
Belgacom	Eaton
BMW Group	Egon Zehnder International
Borealis	EMC Corporation
British American Tobacco	Ericsson
Bunge	Ernst & Young
Canon	Europcar
Carlsberg A/S	EXL Service
CEMEX	FedEx
Chevron	Firmenich SA
Ciba Specialty Chemicals Inc.	Fortis nv
Cloetta Fazer AB (publ)	Fujitsu
CMS Legal Services EEIG	Georg Fischer AG
Coca-Cola HBC, SA	Glitnir Bank
Cochlear	GMAC International Corporation
Companhia Vale do Rio Doce	Grundfos Group
Confederation of Danish Industries	Grupo Votorantim
Considium Consulting Group A/S	Heineken NV
	Henkel KGAA
CTAG	Hilti AG
Dampskibsselskabet "NORDEN" A/S	Hilton International
	Hitachi Ltd.
Danfoss AS	I.M. Skaugen ASA
Danisco	ICI plc
Danske Bank	ING
Degussa AG	International Finance Corporation (IFC)
Det Norske Veritas	ISS A/S
Dexia Group	Itochu Corporation
DONG Energy A/S	J. Lauritzen A/S

Table 2.1 (*cont.*)

Japan Tobacco International	RWE Group
José de Mello (SGPS) SA	Sara Lee DE
Jotun A/S	Scandinavian Tobacco
Khazanah Nasional Berhad	Schindler Management AG
Kongsberg Gruppen ASA	Schlumberger Limited
KPMG	Scottish & Newcastle plc
LEGO Group	SEB-Skandinaviska Enskilda
Lombard Odier Darier Hentsch &	Banken
Cie	Securities Commission
Luxottica Medtronic Inc.	Malaysia
Manpower	Sharp Corporation
Metso Corporation	Shiseido Company Limited
MOBINIL	Siemens
MTN-Mobile Telephone	Sika AG
Networks	Sime Darby Berhad
Nilfisk-Advance	SITA
Norske Skogindustrier ASA	Skanska AB
Numico nv	State Farm Insurance
OMV Aktiengesellschaft	Companies
Outokumpu	Statoil ASA
Panasonic Europe Ltd.	Straumann Holding AG
Pepsico Inc.	Swiss Life
Philip Morris International	Syngenta AG
PPR Pinault-Printemps-Redoute	Tate & Lyle plc
SA	Telefonica SA
PubliGroupe	The Boeing Company
Puig Corporation	The Coca-Cola Company
Rabobank Group	The Dow Chemical Company
Randstad Holding nv	Tietoenator Corporation
Robert Bosch GmbH	Toyota Motor Europe
Rockwool International A/S	Turkcell Communications
RPG Enterprises	Union Bancaire Privée

Table 2.1 (*cont.*)

UPM-Kymmene Corporation	Wallenius Wilhelmsen
Uponor	WILD
Visa International	Wolseley plc
Vitro Corporativo SA de CV	Yazaki Corporation
Vodafone Group Services Ltd.	

A promising area for expanding a business school's academic value-creation, revenue generation and learning partnership activities might lie in executive coaching. There are many definitions of executive coaching, but Kilburg's seems particularly comprehensive:

> Executive coaching is defined as helping relationships form between a client who has managerial authority and responsibility in an organization, and a consultant who uses a wide variety of behavioral techniques and methods to assist the client to achieve a mutually identified set of goals to improve his or her professional performance and personal satisfaction, and consequently to improve the effectiveness of the client's organization with a formally defined coaching agreement.[17]

This definition has several implications:

- Coaches might typically be more loosely associated members of a business school's organization. They are generally independent entrepreneurs who do not want to be part of a business school on a full-time basis. For them, having the freedom to stay away from organizational politics (as they might see it) or stakeholder constraints would be critical. The individual coach would thus be more analogous to a "practice professor" than to a full-time academic member of the staff.

---

[17] R. R. Kilburg, *Executive coaching: Developing managerial wisdom in a world of chaos* (Washington, DC: American Psychological Association, 2000).

- The coaching relationship must be seen as beneficial to both the individual senior executives – so that they can become more effective leaders when dealing with interpersonal issues – and to the corporation as a whole. There should thus be a clear benefit from coaching in terms of bottom-line impacts on the "client's" organization. This bottom-line emphasis seems particularly critical – coaching is not meant to be "a good thing on its own." Instead, it should truly advance organizational performance and have a clear bottom-line effect.
- Coaching is typically a multidisciplinary set of activities. There can be different coaches with different backgrounds. One issue, therefore, would be to develop a base for a more sophisticated dialogue between various types of coaches, an integrative approach within an academic institution. Some coaches, for instance, might come from a more behavioral perspective. Others might address the task with a more macro-oriented focus. Several approaches can be valid. The key is to make sure that there is a dialogue and common understanding to enhance complementarity.
- Enjoying the brand name of an academic institution might also be important for a coach because being affiliated with a good business school typically has some value. The issue is how such an affiliation can be managed for the benefit of the organization itself. Coaches must fulfill their role within the overall value-creation of the academic institution, and not "abuse" the value of the academic institution.[18]

Coaching, thus, can represent an interesting way for a business school to broaden its revenue-generating base by adding new sources of academic value-creation. In all of these instances, a business school's faculty can be leveraged by soliciting the services of independent, freestanding coaches. The school's own faculty should, of course, be fully in charge of all coaching projects, but independent coaches, who

---

[18] M. Sanson, "Executive coaching: An international analysis of the supply of executive coaching services," Doctoral dissertation, University of St. Gallen (2006).

typically command a lower salary, can undertake a significant part of the program delivery, thereby leveraging the school's own permanent, and typically more expensive, faculty.

There are at least three models for creating additional coaching-driven academic value – through in-company programs, open-enrollment programs and on a case-by-case basis:

1. A particular company may see a need to strengthen its leaders to be more effective in core interpersonal issues, including how to lead more effectively, how to work more proactively in teams, how to deal with conflict resolution, how to give to-the-point feedback, and the like. A professor might provide sessions on these themes and relate them to the company's specific situation. Coaches might then work with the participants – individually as well as in small groups – on how these capabilities are practiced and how they can be further strengthened by the participants.

2. Managers from a variety of companies tend to face similar leadership issues to those outlined above. A manager may be strong on several dimensions, but may have an interpersonal style that works against him or her. In this case, an open-enrollment program might be ideal with an emphasis on outdoor exercises – led by coaches – to enhance an individual's capability of working with others, including strengthening his or her introspective insights. The professor would provide the conceptual framework, which would be backed up by support from coaches.

3. Coaching might also be seen as a potentially important element of both open-enrollment programs and company-specific, tailored programs – on an individual basis. In both types of programs, there may be participants who need additional support – to help with their interpersonal management style, for example – whereas others do not. Coaches could be made available for those who need it, and the number of sessions could vary on a case-by-case basis. Thus, because of the availability of personal coaches, most of the participants' needs could be met. It goes without saying that a program must be of at least some minimum

length to provide a meaningful platform for this type of coaching support.

Value-creation through executive coaching at IMD

In terms of support for a particular company, IMD has run a tailored ten-day program for Sara Lee since 1999 with thirty to thirty-five participants per session under the leadership of Jack Wood. He has selected a group of six coaches, who work with him on a continuing basis, and he also provides new knowledge inputs to the coaches, through special sessions for them. The result is a cadre of coaches that work as a team, with clear consistency in quality and a strong knowledge of the client company, Sara Lee.

At the open-enrollment program level, we offer a two-week public program called Mobilizing People. Preston Bottger has led the program from 2001 to 2008, and the stable team of coaches provides support for outdoor activities, above all. As a result, the coaches are being provided with evolving, cutting-edge insights into how individual leadership dimensions can be improved, and their commitment to IMD and to the Mobilizing People program remains strong.

Individual coaching at IMD is offered to participants attending the school's ten-week Program for Executive Development (PED), as well to participants in its one-year MBA program. The coaches are "assigned" by the full-time faculty and program director to participants who need this form of additional support. The participants pay, on an individual basis, for the coaching support required/demanded.

IMD is now focusing explicitly on the further training and development of its coaches. Jack Wood, for instance, has developed an ongoing learning program for the coaches who work with him. At INSEAD, Manfred Kets de Vries has developed a formal program for this. While this program is not mandatory

---

for IMD's coaches, an in-house development program exists, and IMD's coaches have IMD's certification.

IMPLICATIONS FOR BUSINESS SCHOOLS

Competition is intensifying and the market is perhaps fragmenting with new entrants such as management consulting firms, corporate universities and others. Learning partners are becoming increasingly more sophisticated, and companies' and managers' expectations are high. So how can business schools compete meaningfully? There are a number of strategies, outlined below, that can be employed to create the dynamic learning experiences that learning partners are looking for.

1. *Top-caliber faculty team:* Without an excellent faculty team, it will be difficult for a business school to compete in the global marketplace. Therefore, it is important to be able to recruit and retain the best professors, no matter where they come from. The professors must be able to work closely with organizations to understand their learning needs and to build programs based on these needs. And they must work with the other members of the faculty team in order to bring a cross-section of experience to bear on behalf of the entire team – "we, we, we" not "me, me, me."

   Above all, each professor must be actively involved in research – at a high-quality level, ideally involving colleagues on occasion, with a focus that ensures it finds its way into the classroom relatively quickly. We are talking about exceptional faculty members – eager to work with colleagues on an eclectic basis, ready to listen to practitioners and to interact in the classroom through effective pedagogy. At the same time, they clearly must also be outstanding academics in their own right, thought leaders in their own academic field. This balance will be a key ingredient – indeed, a critical premise – for the modern type of academic value-creation we are calling for.

This focus on newness through current research, and the integrity and freedom with regard to what is being taught, is a major competitive advantage for business schools *vis-à-vis* new entrants in the executive education market.

2. *Top-caliber participants:* Those enrolled in programs must ideally have strong intellectual capabilities along with rich cultural and experiential backgrounds. And they must be prepared to share their prescriptive experiences in the classroom – they must be prepared to give and take, to listen and learn – so that two-way learning can take place. Everyone should thus benefit from the new insights that are gained, in the true spirit of lead and be led.

   No one can of course guess *a priori* who will be world class. Even with the best admissions practices, it is hard to assess this beforehand. But diversity seems to be a key factor, as well as attracting intellectually active participants – i.e. interested and interesting!

   The term "participant" has been used rather broadly here. It also applies to the selection of Learning Network companies, which also should be world class.

3. *Real-world academic value-creating context:* The faculty must divide their time between teaching, carrying out research and perhaps, on a limited basis, acting as discussion partners with major companies in various industries. Research and teaching materials should largely be inspired by the business world to ensure that faculty members remain firmly on top of the latest developments in managerial practice. This means that to perform these tasks, research and teaching materials must typically be multidisciplinary in nature. Perhaps the best way to achieve this is to bring forward research-based thought leadership propositions, for further dialogue with practicing managers, as discussed earlier. Faculty can then draw on this experience to create a particularly effective learning environment that might be highly conducive to tackling the critical dilemmas facing businesses today. Thus, this sets the realistic context.

Clearly, the faculty must be of top caliber. And they must be curious, inspiring and challenging! They must be able to add thought leadership. Having gone through a well-established PhD program could definitely be an advantage, as it would provide indoctrination to an intellectually stimulating environment. However, if this results in an axiomatic bent, then the faculty candidate would probably not be able to contribute to the kind of academic value-creation called for here.

4. *Global perspective:* Executive education is becoming more international and – with organizations' growing interest in cultural issues – those schools that succeed in offering a truly global experience across all their programs and activities will have a significant competitive advantage. But this requires a strong faculty and participant base, an excellent school reputation and financial resources. For companies competing in the global marketplace, where the boundaries between geographic markets are blurring, it is increasingly important that at least some business schools have exactly this rich international mix of participants, faculty and teaching and research materials. What this perhaps means, above all, is a focus on key dilemmas, rather than pursuing specific, often nation-based, "answers." But, as noted, only relatively few business schools will play in this top league – the rest will remain local.

5. *Two-way learning:* Business schools must make sure that professors are active in research, a key argument shared so far. Further, they must present their ideas in a pedagogically meaningful way. As noted, lecturing alone, as a one-way process, cannot accomplish the juxtaposition of propositional and prescriptive sources of knowledge that is required for two-way, lead and be led learning. Professors must more readily try to adopt an approach that encourages learning through discussion and the real-world application of leading-edge concepts. To accomplish this, faculty must engage and interact with participants and companies – listen, understand and put themselves in their context. The participants

must also listen and engage, by sharing their knowledge and insights in the classroom. A learning process based on open-minded participation, frank interaction and action learning is likely to result in an immediate and tangible application of ideas for learning partners.

6. *Virtuous cycle of value-creation:* Business schools must nurture the symbiotic relationship between each of the components in the value-creation cycle – research, the MBA degree programs, executive programs and company collaboration (see Figure 2.1). This includes action-research, projects and focus on key managerial issues. Faculty must be able to interact with senior executives on an ongoing basis through executive programs and other collaborations with business (e.g. case writing, Learning Network) and bring this experience back into both the MBA classroom and the executive education classroom. But this requires focus on the areas to be developed – only those that can provide the basis for good two-way academic value-creation should be pursued. Strategy means choice.

To guide this, one should only settle for learning opportunities that can provide a "global meeting place" setting with a truly diverse set of top caliber participants. A "real world, real learning" focus – on essential managerial problems that are of interest to researchers and practicing managers alike – is also essential. The learning opportunity should also have a "lifelong learning" focus, so that the value-creating dialogue between practitioners and professors continues after the participants have completed their specific course. More basic management programs, which try to bring across fundamental theories and practice at the introductory stage, would typically not lend themselves to such cutting-edge academic value-creation. This is the dilemma for many business schools with large undergraduate programs in business – these basic activities take up so much of the faculty's time and energy that the basic lead and be led value-creation often suffers. The fact that these large undergraduate programs often also serve as financial "cash cows" for many schools does not make this issue any easier to get around.

And as we have discussed, value-creation does not only take place through the research–classroom interface – but also, more broadly, through a formal learning network and through coaching.

7. *Incorporate different paradigms for academic value-creation:* It seems important to be open to testing out entirely new value paradigms at the business school. For instance, IMD's learning from leading ballet companies, i.e. how they create a culture that is both "we, we, we" *and* "me, me, me" – a joint workshop on this was held at IMD on January 30, 2007.

Another example might be to examine the integration of different practices from design. This would call for "a designer school approach" in defining, analyzing and operationalizing actions. At the World Economic Forum in Davos in 2007, several "design school" workshops that focused on the use of designer practices were offered.[19] Strong links to the design school tradition can be found when it comes to building on particular aspects of practice, as is done in several professional academic disciplines, such as medical schools,[20] engineering schools,[21] law schools[22] or education schools.[23] All have a strong focus on design by building on one's understanding of particular cases and then generalizing from this.

In a nutshell, all of this has *one* overriding implication for business schools: They must be world class in every aspect – top-caliber faculty

---

[19] *forumblog.org* (World Economic Forum, 2007), wef.typepad.com/blog/, accessed June 13, 2007.

[20] W. G. Rothstein, *American medical schools and the practice of medicine: A history* (New York: Oxford University Press, 1987).

[21] T. S. Reynolds, *The engineer in America: A historical anthology from technology and culture* (Chicago, IL: University of Chicago Press, 1991); J. J. Duderstadt, *A university for the 21st century* (Ann Arbor, MI: University of Michigan Press, 2000).

[22] J. W. Hurst, *The growth of American law: The law makers* (Union, NJ: Lawbook Exchange, 2001).

[23] D. F. Labaree, *The trouble with ed schools* (New Haven, CT: Yale University Press, 2004).

doing top-caliber research and top pedagogical delivery, top-caliber participants, top-caliber global context, top-caliber two-way learning between the faculty and the participants – and in the end this will result in a top-caliber cycle of academic value-creation!

IMD's real world, real learning global meeting place

To serve the growing demand for international leadership skills, IMD bases its mission on a couple of important premises – "real world, real learning" and the "global meeting place."

Roger Schmenner, a faculty member from Indiana University who has spent a total of four years at IMD as a visiting professor, sums up how IMD is a truly global business school. In the following excerpt, he shares with us how value-creation in a global context takes place at IMD:

"As business schools go, it is hard to find a more international place . . . The vast majority of the school's revenues come from either open-enrollment executive courses or company-specific courses. Most of these are of one or two weeks in duration, with some longer and some merely a day or two. The executives who turn up for the courses come from all over the globe. . .

Given the diversity, and [IMD's] location in Switzerland, a country of four official languages for its 7 million residents, the most salient characteristic of the place is that there is no dominant culture. Everyone here is a minority. The working language is English, and native speakers have some inherent advantages that way, but the English here is as likely to be spoken with a South Asian accent as a US one. US multinationals are among the companies that form the backbone of IMD's network of sponsoring companies [IMD's Learning Network], but they are a minority as well.

Over the years, IMD has developed some traits that make it easy for the various minorities to feel comfortable and productive. IMD is a big proponent of the case method and it has written a host of the very best teaching cases set internationally.

Thus, the spotlight for any day's classes is constantly shifting from one area of the world to another. Increasingly, many of the cases have associated videos so that everyone can take a brief tour of the case setting and see the managers at the center of the case on their home turf.

Often, before a case is discussed in class, it is the topic for small group study. These small groups are typically very hetero-geneous, and commonly it is in these small groups where the different cultures collide. Participants learn much as they try to argue their points with others of a completely different turn of mind . . ."[24]

---

[24] R. Schmenner, "IMD's real world, real learning global meeting place." *Indiana University CIBER Newsletter* (Spring, 2002).

3 The critical role of R&D

The world is cross functional. In the pharmaceutical industry – and I am sure this applies to many other industries as well – different disciplines have to work together to create a product that prevents or cures a disease or improves quality of life. In our programs – mostly customized programs – we expect the faculty to work together the same way we expect our scientists to work across disciplinary boundaries. Scientific thinking must lead to application for it to have any value, in companies as well as in business schools.

Jürgen Brokatzky-Geiger,[1]
Head of Human Resources and
Member of the Executive Committee, Novartis

For us, academic research in itself is not that important. Much more germane is what can be applied to real life situations. It is like the technology of a car: When you drive a car, you want the instruments to be correct and you want certain comfort features. You don't really care about the research that went into it. What you care about is the user-friendliness and relevance of the output.

Nick Shreiber[2]

KEY POINTS

- Strong, practitioner-oriented research is the basis of all meaningful academic value-creation. This thought leadership must find its way into a business school's programs – fast!
- It is the *interface* between propositional knowledge – in the form of practitioner-relevant research put forward by faculty – and prescriptive knowledge – representing "real practice" put forward by leading practitioners from corporations all over the

---

[1] As quoted in P. Lorange, "A performance-based, minimalist human resource management approach in business schools," *Human Resource Management* (published online November 21, 2006), 649–658.
[2] Former CEO of Tetra Pak, as quoted in B. Büchel and D. Antunes, "Reflections on executive education: The users' and providers' perspectives," *Academy of Management Learning and Education* 6 (September 2007).

world – that leads to strong, grounded theory-building research progress.[3]

- Much of this research will be cross-disciplinary and eclectic in nature – in contrast with more traditional, axiomatic and discipline-based research, which is perhaps less dominant and less effective than before as a source of inspiration for new knowledge for the learning partnership.
- Neither undergraduate nor PhD program activities will typically add significant value to the research-based discovery process. This is due to the inexperience of undergraduate students and their lack of prescriptive insights and the axiomatic focus of most doctoral programs.

INTRODUCTION

It is critical that business schools invest in fresh research that is aligned with the needs of companies rather than primarily in "conventional" research that may be too esoteric in nature, too narrowly focused, too driven by a single discipline, and too axiomatic. Why? Because companies want research that provides insights into their business issues – research that is both empirically driven and real-world in context. In order to reflect reality, it is often also imperative that the research is international in scope and meets the cross-cultural demands of many real business situations. In short, research must lead to propositions that are at the forefront of current and evolving business issues.

The long-standing philosophy that good research must have a heavy emphasis on axiomatic, disciplinary thinking, with hypothesis testing and refutation of truths, is increasingly being replaced by a lead and be led research philosophy. Academics, through their research, might come up with propositions that represent cutting-edge thinking. However, it must be articulated and presented in such a

---

[3] J. Mokyr, *The gifts of Athena* (Princeton, NJ: Princeton University Press, 2002);
B. G. Glaser and A. L. Strauss, *The discovery of grounded theory: Strategies for qualitative research* (Chicago, IL: Aldine, 1967).

way that it can be understood by leading practitioners, who can then express their views on it – their prescriptive knowledge. It is this interaction between propositional and prescriptive knowledge that often leads to additional insights for all. For researchers, this means a unique way to develop their research insights further – logical incrementalism, grounded theory building.[4]

Integrative thinking is key here! One of the most critical features of IMD is the strong emphasis on interpreting various domain-specialized trains of thought and specific knowledge. Our ability to pull concepts together is more important than to pull them apart! This can be seen as a hallmark for much of the research that is going on at IMD, as well as for much of the interactive learning!

Typically, traditional business models tend to be soundly grounded in the culture of the host country. This, however, can prevent a company from discovering new, alternative ways of doing business based on insights from other cultures or in other parts of the world. In line with Mokyr's thinking,[5] the challenge for business schools is to bring cutting-edge new research thought together with the best practitioners, probably from several different countries, who might be open to new interpretations of their business rationales – their prescriptive knowledge. In this way, the business model might continually evolve and expand with research-based propositional knowledge meeting prescriptive knowledge in an international context. Take, for example, the quest to understand how to do business in China. By bringing the latest thoughts and insights on China into the classroom, the constant interaction between academics and practitioners – in overlapping fields and from many countries and cultures – enriches the research and provides the basis for true thought leadership.

In this chapter, we will explore the critical factors that contribute to relevant thought leadership and how these can help business schools' learning partners make the most of the opportunities available to them.

---

[4] Glaser and Strauss, *The discovery of grounded theory.*
[5] Mokyr, *The gifts of Athena.*

Then, we shall further explore how propositional knowledge – research – can meet prescriptive knowledge – from practical experience.

CREATING AN ENVIRONMENT FOR THOUGHT LEADERSHIP

Clearly, it is particularly important that business school research, which is characterized by the competence base of the faculty, is strong. It must represent sound propositional thinking. As we have noted, the value created by the research is greatly enhanced by discussions in the classroom, where cross-sections of leading practitioners bring their prescriptive knowledge to bear. As a result, the faculty members often gain additional insights from the discussions with participants who have real-world experiences in many different industries and cultural settings.

Many schools work with a business model that is based on large-scale teaching programs. The downside of such a large-scale focus can be that it is more difficult to adopt and integrate (and then update again) new research findings. Large MBA programs, for instance, encompassing many parallel sections, are not as well equipped as smaller programs to adopt new materials quickly because of the extensive coordination costs of doing so. Smaller flexible programs can incorporate new materials much more easily and speedily. Again, the cycle time – from research to class and, finally, to application – is key. If this is not fast enough, the quality of the interaction between propositional and prescriptive knowledge might suffer.

A similar argument can be made if much of the academic teaching focus is on undergraduates, who tend to have less clarity in their prescriptive knowledge bases, simply due to their lack of experience. Again, the quality of the lead and be led interface might suffer. Ironically, the same can be said about many PhD programs. The candidates in these programs – strong as their intellectual powers undoubtedly are – will typically not have the prescriptive insights to put forward from cutting-edge practice, and axiomatic narrowness can "blindfold" them. Paradoxically, PhD programs can thus set back the scientific value-creating process, rather than advance it.

It is equally important that the research is relevant *and* that the propositional knowledge is accessible to executives and organizations so that faculty can be in meaningful contact with them to address emerging business issues based on an exchange of ideas. Without this contact, it would be difficult for faculty to come up with new conceptual insights that would be further improved by senior executives. The research should thus typically be cross disciplinary in nature to enhance its practical relevance. Business problems and opportunities do not usually present themselves in neat functional packages, e.g. as a finance, accounting or marketing problem or opportunity. Instead, real-life business dilemmas almost always involve a variety of functional areas that must be addressed simultaneously. Prescriptive knowledge from practice typically reflects this and – to be compatible – the propositional knowledge from research should also do so.

An example of cross-disciplinary research at IMD comes from the project led by Dan Denison and John Ward, specialists in organizational behavior and strategy/family business, respectively. It had long been assumed that family-owned firms would not perform as well, on average, as publicly traded firms. By combining a database to assess effective corporate culture with performance data on both family-dominated and public firms, the professors were able to come up with empirical results that seem to suggest strongly the opposite of the conventional wisdom: Well-managed family-owned firms tend to *outperform* publicly traded ones![6] It took two researchers from very different backgrounds, with truly separate frames of reference to come up with this. By combining forces, they were able to think outside the box.

Most business schools have already made the shift toward more dynamic learning and more action-oriented research. A focus on projects and real issues has become increasingly key. Research output relating to current issues is more beneficial to corporations in their efforts to formulate successful strategies. Business schools should of

---

[6] D. Denison, C. Lief and J. Ward, "Culture in family-owned enterprises: Recognizing and leveraging unique strengths," *Family Business Review* 17 (March 2004).

course also make sure that this type of applicable research output reaches its learning partners as early as possible.

THE IMPORTANCE OF EXPERIMENTATION

Academic institutions, as noted, are often inherently conservative with their longstanding practices for creating academic value. More experimentation in alternative ways of delivering academic value is called for! For example, parallel organizational forms might be developed via experimentation. At Wharton, for instance, the school wanted to accelerate the international dimension in its MBA program. In order to do this, it developed the so-called Lauder Institute, together with the rest of the University of Pennsylvania, where students would get *both* an MBA degree with a focus on international business *and* an MA degree in a particular language, coupled with historical and political science insights for the given country of choice. Over time, the pioneering efforts at the Lauder Institute "trickled down" into the ordinary MBA program. This experiment and the creation of a parallel organization definitely led to a speedier internationalization of the original organizational entity.

Similar examples can certainly be found at IMD too. The establishment of research centers in Shanghai and Mumbai (described in more detail later in the chapter), for instance, have led to an additional focus on IMD's research regarding China and India in general. The creation of the Orchestrating Winning Performance Program (OWP) has led to more cross-disciplinary program development and teaching. And, those programs with an action orientation have had positive effects on the more traditional programs. Specifically a new breed of action-oriented programs was created, based on a methodology developed by Peter Killing, Thomas Malnight and others, with their emphasis on "must-win battles."[7] This action-oriented learning seems to have led subsequently to a revitalization of other parts of

---

[7] J. P. Killing, T. Malnight and T. Keys, *Must-win battles: How to win them, again and again* (Upper Saddle River, NJ: Wharton School Publishing, 2006).

IMD's portfolio. Again, the creation of "parallel organizations and experimentation" led to a speeding up of innovation.

ALTERNATIVE CHANNELS FOR RAPID DISSEMINATION

The classic channels for disseminating research – refereed, discipline-based, axiomatic journals – are perhaps not as well suited to the rapid, broad-based dissemination of new knowledge that is called for today. The refereeing and scholarly journal-based publication process alone can take as long as three to five years! Additionally, the more eclectic topics, relevant to practicing managers, are often less appealing to typical axiomatic journals. As Starkey and Tiratsoo put it in their recent work, *The business school and the bottom line*, "When it comes to research . . . [business schools] are confronted by a culture and an incentive system that hardly seem to recognize the practitioner at all."[8] Consequently, we might need to look for new, broader outlets for disseminating some of these cutting-edge research outputs in order to ensure that they are still fresh when they reach fellow academics and practicing managers.

Research monographs, edited books, other more popular print or online publications such as newspapers, the business school's own website and even webcasts might increasingly become alternative ways to disseminate research. But the general conservatism of the academic profession can lead to friction here. When it comes to faculty appointments, promotions, tenure decisions and the like, it is often the case that single-authored articles, published in traditional refereed journals, are seen as representing higher quality research. This traditional method of assessing faculty performance can discourage faculty from producing more modern, relevant and cross-functional research. And if relevance is overlooked, this can easily mean that the propositional knowledge has not interacted with the prescriptive knowledge. It might be argued, therefore, that

---

[8] K. Starkey and N. Tiratsoo, *The business school and the bottom line* (Cambridge: Cambridge University Press, 2007).

traditional axiomatic research may in fact often be *less* cutting edge!

In my experience, many (not all) tenure-track and tenured faculty members at business schools tend to be rather risk averse – at times more risk averse than the students they teach. This causes significant cognitive dissonance in the classroom. Worse for faculty management, however, is the fact that senior tenured faculty members can be more risk averse than those, often untenured, junior and senior faculty members who are engaged in truly cutting-edge work. Consciously or subconsciously, risk-averse senior faculty members might end up torpedoing work that is somewhat outside of the norm. Consequently, promising and pioneering junior faculty members can either regress to the mean – or leave. The challenge (and opportunity) for IMD is to identify those faculty members who fit IMD's needs and who are unhappy about the risk profile and intellectual narrow-mindedness of their colleagues at other schools and, then, aggressively attempt to court these candidates.

The true breakthroughs and benefits for learning partners will be achieved if the applicable research output is disseminated through teaching, discussions and other channels, such as *ad hoc* seminars. This might generally take place via several "meeting places" and thus lead to an open dialogue with a wider constituency of stakeholders, i.e. a give-and-take process, learning for all. The key is that the research must be conducted in an open context, exposed to as many as possible, so that maximum feedback and a multitude of eclectic inputs can be brought to bear.

Examples of IMD's channels for rapid distribution

As previously described, IMD disseminates its research to practicing managers via a number of the Learning Network's activities – weekly webcasts, CEO Roundtables and the like. And while the school does publish in some conventional vehicles (e.g. 21 academic/refereed articles in 2006), it also publishes a number of books and cases that are typically available to practicing managers while the research is still fresh. For example, in 2006, 15 books and reports were published, 35 book chapters/contributions, 114 managerial or newspaper articles (including articles published in print and web-based media), 11 *Perspectives for Managers* and 23 IMD working papers. In terms of teaching material, 132 case studies were written, several of which included teaching notes and videos; much of this material is distributed throughout the world via case clearing houses, such as ECCH.

In addition to the above activities, IMD regularly works with a number of leading business publications to ensure its latest thinking is made available to practicing managers in a timely fashion. Two in particular come to mind:

- *Financial Times*: Every year the *Financial Times* (FT) calls for contributions to its "FT Mastering Series." Several of IMD's faculty members have had articles published as part of this series. The FT is read by more UK senior business people than any other daily newspaper, and through the FT newspaper and FT.com, these articles can be accessed by more than 400,000 leading executives in the UK.[9] IMD faculty members regularly receive positive feedback from people who have read their articles, along with suggestions for further developing the research.
- *Business Life* – British Airways in-flight magazine is dedicated to the business traveler. Several IMD professors are publishing a column – on a regular basis – again with positive feedback from the readership of more than 100,000.

IMD also releases some key research findings online twice a week via the "Tomorrow's Challenges" articles. Each one is read by 2,000 to 3,000 people and popularity continues to grow.

---

[9] FT.com website, www.fttoolkit.co.uk/advertising/framework.html, accessed January 30, 2007.

Once a month, the "Tomorrow's Challenges" are included in IMD's Webletter, which is sent by e-mail to more than 90,000 subscribers.

INVESTING IN RESEARCH

Of course, the cost of good academic research tends to be very expensive. How can a business school afford this? Executive education, as I indicated in Chapter 2, might provide a means of paying for the research. This assumes, however, that the research can be linked to the types of activities going on in executive education, i.e. that propositional thought leadership, stemming from research, can in fact meet prescriptive knowledge from practitioners in executive education classes. This implies that there typically would have to be some relevance requirements on the research – it must have at least a minimum of interest for practice.

We may also see the equivalent of a Baumol–Bowen effect here, where the technological advances tend to lead to higher costs, but the price increases that can be levied to cover these advances typically do not have a high enough impact to compensate for their entire cost.[10] Thus, technological advances, in the end, may lead to a decrease in the level of profitability and a flattening out of the wealth generation capabilities that are available to a firm. A similar effect can perhaps be seen when it comes to research beyond certain limits within business schools.

To some extent, the price of executive programs can be increased to reflect the latest thinking and the potential benefits that the participants may get from cutting-edge thought leadership. There are, however, limits to these price increases. In the end, it boils down to a judgment call on the part of the business school leadership. Because of the constantly evolving business environment, there will never be a clear-cut line between the type of research that is directly applicable

---

[10] W. Baumol and W. Bowen, *Performing arts: The economic dilemma* (New York: 20th Century Fund, 1966).

to business and those research activities that might have a longer-term – and perhaps more uncertain – payoff. Nevertheless, some of this "seemingly less relevant" research is also necessary. This is a balancing act that makes it all the more important for a business school to be in constant contact and dialogue with its learning partners to keep abreast of their ongoing and even future research needs. The ability to see opportunities before others truly comes to the fore here (see Chapter 8).

IMD's investment in research centers in Shanghai and Mumbai

IMD's research centers in Asia are good examples of how IMD is investing in research that responds to the needs of its learning partners. In order to do more research on this key economic growth region, IMD has established a research center in Shanghai and has attracted two outstanding Chinese professors. The school has also set up a similar center in Mumbai, India, and is also considering a new research center for Latin America.

The choice of a location for the Latin American research center could pose a dilemma. If Mexico City is chosen, for instance, it might be difficult to attract executives and research focus relating to major South American countries, such as Brazil, Argentina, Chile, etc. If Sao Paolo is chosen, conversely it might be difficult to attract people from Mexico. Thus, a location in Miami might be realistic – many Latin American businesses do have strong links with Miami. Over time, it might be natural to relocate the research center if activities should gravitate heavily toward one country or region.

Having these research centers *in situ* will hopefully allow IMD to better understand cutting-edge local issues and collaborate with business in these regions. Presence leads to added credibility with local business!

These centers will also stimulate professors to generate fresh new concepts that can be applied quickly in the classroom, as well as to develop relevant case studies and other teaching materials. And, above all, they will facilitate a better understanding of the key leadership practices coming from these two cultures, especially in light of the fact that just over one-quarter of IMD's activities are with executives and firms of Asian origin. By bringing the research generated through these research centers back to IMD – the global meeting place – it will enable us to help our learning partners learn more about doing business in these key economic growth regions of the world. And when managers from these regions attend IMD programs, we will be able to help them learn more about doing business in other parts of the world.

Each of these research centers is rather small – as they are intended to operate more or less on a virtual basis. Only a few research associates and secretaries are there permanently. Faculty come and go. They benefit from the local contacts and the lower set-up costs in doing China- or India-based research, given the fact that much can be arranged for them beforehand. The research is then brought back to the "global meeting place" i.e. IMD in Lausanne. Thus, IMD's focus is on one campus, but with a number of physically small research centers, to speed up the global discovery process.

TEACHING AND RESEARCH

So far, in this book, I have maintained that research and teaching go hand in hand. Many academic institutions, however, make a three-point distinction between basic research, applied research and teaching. In my opinion, this is a false distinction. First of all, the research side (let us argue the applied research side for now) must be closely related to teaching, i.e. its results must be part of the classroom, and the dialogue between conceptual and practical thinking must be vibrant – a key to learning for all. Thus, the research is actually being tested in an effective way and on an ongoing basis *vis-à-vis* the practical outside world. There is perhaps no more effective way of testing new thoughts than to bring them into the "global meeting place." The feedback is instant!

Let us illustrate this with an example based on the research on growth undertaken by Bala Chakravarthy and the author.[11] After examining a database containing more than 4,500 observations of growth over a 10-year period, conducting a set of structural interviews and looking at several case studies, we came up with the following propositions. Growth can best be pursued by building on established business strengths, not only by using these strengths to explore new markets or as a basis for adding new capabilities, but also by adopting a planned "two-step" strategic move. Thus, a company might first enter a new market before adding new capabilities tailored to that particular market, or vice versa, i.e. the company would first develop new capabilities for its present customer base, and then take these into new markets.

When we first presented these propositions on effective growth in the classroom, based on our research thus far, the participants noted that management – the actors behind the research into, say, new product development – would be as important as the researchers themselves. To make things happen, it would be necessary to have internal entrepreneurs, supported by senior executives as well as top management. And these key roles would take on different colors in different cultural settings. The end result was that our view on growth was greatly enriched through the prescriptive inputs from the class on the need to consider key actors in the growth equation. All of us gained additional insights – logical incrementalism from a research-based point of view.[12]

So, what is the role of basic research? In my opinion, basic research and applied research go together. A focus on basic research alone, without the link to the classroom, and ultimately practice, is,

<hr>

[11] B. Chakravarthy and P. Lorange, *Profit or growth? Why you don't have to choose* (Philadelphia, PA: Wharton/Pearson, 2007).
[12] Glaser and Strauss, *The discovery of grounded theory.*

I believe, hard to support. It becomes difficult to maintain relevance in such isolated circumstances. In this regard, the French pure mathematicians of two centuries ago spring to mind. They purified the science of pure mathematics to such an extent that it was "beautiful," but it became increasingly irrelevant to all and consequently lost its broader appeal for other intellectuals. In the end, it was merely a small clique of pure mathematicians who talked to each other. By contrast, prominent present-day social scientists, such as Gibbons and colleagues, see academic work as moving from academic isolation toward more integration of science in society.[13] Such integration would presumably mean that the best prescriptive knowledge from leading business sources would be more accepted in academia too.

Recent developments within the field of research and development seem to indicate that there is more of a seamless process and that the distinction between basic research and the subsequent application-oriented development seems to be fading.[14] Research is now much more linked to end-user applications, and it is typically more incremental. Large new research breakthroughs, essentially decoupled from the need for constant improvements by the customer, seem to be rare. More research productivity is called for. Rapid innovations dominate – relatively small and practical, focused on how to do things better from the customer's viewpoint. The process of research and development is now *one*, rather than segmented. This continuity applies to business schools and their learning partners too. The development of new knowledge will typically be rather incremental in nature. Learning partners are not calling for major research breakthroughs – they are not expecting quantum leaps in thought leadership.

---

[13] M. Gibbons, C. Limoges, S. Nowotny, P. Scott and M. Trow, *The new production of knowledge: The dynamics of science and research in contemporary societies* (London: Sage, 1994).

[14] "The rise and fall of corporate R&D: Out of the dusty labs," *The Economist* (March 3, 2007).

The key, therefore, is to see research – basic and applied – as one process, the aim of which is to come up with new propositional knowledge that can then be brought to the classroom for rapid testing with cross-sections of leading practitioners. There is not much room, in my opinion, for a lot of basic research *per se* in academic communities such as professional business schools. At IMD, the "What to do Next" internet-based simulation conceived by Stuart Read and Willem Smit is a good example of how field research has been translated into useful results. Developed to be both an effective learning tool that could offer participants real-time feedback and a means of collecting data on how corporate managers react when presented with specific situations involving uncertainty, the realistic simulation is a real example of a virtuous cycle of positive feedback. The data collected during the game is being translated into publications for practice that, in turn, will be brought back into the classroom. The experiential expertise that emerges during classroom discussions provides another benefit for the researchers as they are constantly introduced to new variables – which might influence how "what to do next?" strategies are used, or where they are effective – and this allows them to generate a new set of hypotheses, which gets fed into the data – and so it continues.[15]

The axiomatic departmental structure that is typical of so many business schools, regrettably, might tend to solidify a focus from the past – in terms of both teaching and research – and will thus perhaps not sufficiently stimulate modern academic value-creation. But, according to *The Economist*, "there is hope for the real world yet." AACSB International (The Association to Advance Collegiate Schools of Business) – the premier accrediting agency for business schools – has come out with a draft report that is "meant to make

---

[15] W. Smit and S. Read, "Late for the train: How framing retards response to environmental change," *2007 INFORMS Marketing Science Conference* (Singapore Management University, Lee Kong Chian School of Business, June 28–30, 2007); W. Smit and S. Read, "When you have a hammer: Corporate managers respond to uncertainty," *36th European Marketing Academy Conference* (Reykjavik University, May 22–25, 2007).

business schools centres of practical research and pedagogy, rather than sanctuaries of disciplined-based scholarship." On top of this, two prominent publications that do MBA rankings – the *Financial Times* and *Business Week* – are now evaluating business schools based on "their contribution to both journals they consider purely 'academic' and ones they consider 'practitioner' – i.e., ones managers might read."[16]

Success lies not so much in the esoteric ideas, but in the impact of the ideas! The quality of the research process can thus be enhanced by "thinking outside the box," so that good propositional knowledge can be produced and be further enhanced through interaction with solid prescriptive knowledge from practice. This lead and be led process is likely to produce better research – and possibly even better teaching!

IMPLICATIONS FOR BUSINESS SCHOOLS

Learning partners are looking for research that addresses their current and future business issues. But, more than that, they want it to be high quality and relevant, and they want it in a timely manner so that they can apply it to the dilemmas they are currently facing. Therefore, a key challenge for business schools is to develop a strong research process, based on relevant propositional insights that have been exposed to a healthy dialogue with prescriptive knowledge from practice. Furthermore, there must be a commitment to rapidly disseminating applicable research. So how can business schools do this? The following strategies are worth considering:

1. *Investment:* Business schools must allocate a high proportion of their spending to research and program development. And research and development costs certainly include faculty time. Without a realistic view on this, which includes a relatively modest teaching load for faculty, there can hardly be much research to feed into the programs to make them cutting edge so that they will generate the

---

[16] "Practically irrelevant?" *The Economist* (August 28, 2007).

funds that in turn will allow business schools to further fund their research and continue to provide a venue for dissemination. Cutting-edge programs draw strong sets of executives, thus allowing the professors to gain valuable feedback that further refines the research agenda. It is thus a virtual, positive cycle. Heavy research commitment allows the school to offer more relevant, incisive thought leadership programs, which in turn attract the best practitioners to the classroom, which ensures *both* a strong economy for the business school *and* strong prescriptive inputs that benefit the research and so on!

2. *Faculty incentives:* As we will discuss in more detail in Chapter 6, it is essential that business schools have a human resources strategy in place that rewards eclectic and action-oriented academic value-creation. As we shall see, it is important that faculty compensation rewards be given for research-based *results*, as opposed to mere plans and promises.

    The link to the teaching side also plays a role here. Faculty typically tend to be rated by the participants based on the quality of each individual session. Some might perhaps find it more advantageous, less risky, to base a session on tried and tested – but older – materials, and even hesitate to bring the latest research into their sessions. This would be dysfunctional. Teaching evaluations must not be conducted in such a way that they end up slowing down the freshness of the research.

    Faculty add different things! Hence, they should be incentivized in different ways – some may want to put relatively more of their focus on research, others on additional teaching, others on "citizenship" tasks, such as working with alumni, etc. Diversity is good – as long as all faculty are incentivized to contribute their best, in whatever ways they are most comfortable. Compensation and incentives must thus be individualized! This becomes particularly important as most faculty members will go through periods in their careers with different emphases – their priorities and interests typically shift over time.

3. *Relevance and a cross-disciplinary approach:* Business school professors must be at the vanguard when it comes to presenting conceptual frameworks based on empirical research – strong propositional knowledge. Eclectic, cross-disciplinary research dealing with real business dilemmas is often of far more value to learning partners than research that is too esoteric or focused on a narrow disciplinary area. And the cutting-edge research insights should be incorporated into the school's broader teaching programs. With the acceleration of knowledge, the only competitive advantage a school will in fact have is to be the fastest to generate new knowledge through research and to incorporate this into its teaching programs – fast. Speed is of the essence!

As noted, the business school must be seen as a meeting place for faculty when it comes to research, with different faculty members having different eclectic angles. Many of these faculty members can come from the school itself or from different academic institutions, which will further enhance cross-fertilization. A good example is the cooperation between the Sloan School at MIT and IMD, where joint research (and executive teaching) are carried out in the areas of innovation management and supply chain management. The two related programs are Driving Strategic Innovation: Faster Innovation across the Value Chain, and Managing the Extended Supply Chain: Beyond Productivity and Efficiency. The combined intellectual resources of Sloan/MIT and IMD have led to a truly strong value-creating thrust – appreciated by the marketplace and academia alike.

Another academic alliance is between IMD and the two Swiss Federal Institutes of Technology – ETH in Zurich and EPFL in Lausanne. For more than ten years, the three institutions have been jointly running the Mastering Technology Enterprise executive program, directed by Ralf Seifert. Recognizing the richness of the start-up experience shared by some of the speakers in the program, he brought together a team of authors from IMD and EPFL to seize this opportunity. The result is a book of more than thirty case studies for which research was gathered in the field.[17] The examples of start-ups – both successful and less successful – cover the entire life cycle of an entrepreneurial venture, from identifying the opportunity, through raising finance, to harvesting. It also includes case research on internal venturing at established companies such as Logitech and Tetra Pak. Not only did the idea for the research emerge from the classroom, but also the interactions within the classroom served to refine and hone it before it was published to benefit an even wider audience.

For IMD, with its focus on eclectic, integrated research and delivery, these alliances serve an important purpose – namely to link IMD more closely to state-of-the-art sources of fundamental disciplines. While IMD represents the antithesis of disciplinary focus, we can still benefit from this, hence, these alliances.

4. *International scope:* It is important to create a "global meeting place," where practitioners from all over the world can come together to offer the highest level of prescriptive knowledge as part of the lead and be led value-creating process. To find a practical site for such a global meeting place is key. Practical access, safety and no bias toward people from certain parts of the world will be key. Regional or even local schools cannot provide the same "global meeting place" environment. Thus, a large country, with its typically rather strong national biases, is probably *not* the best location for a truly international business school. What *is* required is stronger thought leadership input, perhaps inspired by research based in China, India, Russia, Latin America (the BRICs) or other emerging economies, for discussion in a global meeting place environment. In this way, non-Chinese executives, for example, will benefit from getting to understand the Chinese perspective on business dilemmas and Chinese executives will benefit from a global perspective. Research institutes should perhaps be located in strategic locations around the world, but for maximum impact,

---

[17] R. Seifert, B. Leleux and C. Tucci (eds.), *Science-based entrepreneurship* (London: Springer, forthcoming).

the output from these institutes should be fed back into one "global meeting place."

5. *Rapid, continuous and applicable:* As noted, the speed at which the research is done and then brought into the classroom is of paramount importance because learning partners want research that deals with real strategic issues in a timely manner and on an ongoing basis. And the various viewpoints from the wide range of participants in the classroom will demonstrate that issues and opportunities can be understood in a variety of ways, i.e. as dilemmas rather than absolute truths.

In order to ensure that they are addressing academia's emerging needs for relevance (yes relevance!), as well as their learning partners' needs for relevant, cutting-edge research that is immediately applicable, business schools must explore channels other than the more academic journals for quickly disseminating their research findings to fellow academics and to practicing managers alike. As noted, this could be through the press, research monographs, edited books, webcasts and the school's own website. A minimalist inner structure within the business school can also ultimately help to speed up the dissemination of research. This could take the form of a smooth, non-bureaucratic process for approving research projects, an easy way to assign research associates and other support to these tasks, and a "light," non-bureaucratic follow-up on research outputs.

6. *Collaboration:* Above all, business schools must develop closer ties with business if they are to remain cutting edge. Partnerships with leading corporations and executives are essential for driving the research agenda, ensuring relevance and challenging the business school to innovate. Long-term relationships of various types are increasingly regarded as essential for both sides. Developing thought leadership and then testing it out on broad-based, cross-cultural, cross-experiential groups of executives is more likely to lead to true research progress. In my opinion, this means that academics are leading practitioners and, at the same time, that

they are being led by them. Propositional and prescriptive knowledge exist in a symbiotic relationship – collaboration between
academia and practice is key for world-class research! And as
IMD's alliances with MIT and EPFL/ETH show, collaboration
with academics from other academic institutions can also bear
fruit, provided that the vital interplay with practice is not
neglected.

7. *Experimentation:* In order to be innovative, business schools need
   to open their minds to alternative ways of creating academic value.
   We have mentioned the "What to do next" game which simulates
   uncertain situations, collects new managerial data based on the
   answers, with the result being the generation of new materials for
   debate in the classroom, the formulation of new hypotheses and so
   on. We have also, in the previous chapter, discussed how to reach
   out for inspiration from other types of institutions, such as design
   schools and even ballet companies. Through these types of experimentation, business schools may thus be in a better position to
   create novel research.

Research and development at IMD

At IMD, research and development expenditure (which includes
faculty time) accounts for about 27 per cent of our total costs.
Creating state-of-the-art research and course material on an
ongoing basis for immediate use in the classroom is an important part of each faculty member's agenda, and the annual
performance assessment reflects this. Only actual published
research output counts, not work in progress. Remuneration, of
course, follows from this.

Faculty work hand in hand with business to produce cross-
functional and cross-disciplinary research, which is reflected in
all our programs and which directly benefits our learning partners. Some examples of IMD research across disciplinary
borders include:

- A professor specializing in organizational culture, Dan Denison, and a leadership professor, Robert Hooijberg, joined forces to research "effectiveness assessments and their relation to hierarchical levels." They examined leadership behaviors that predict which effectiveness criteria to use at various hierarchical levels, and how hierarchical relationships affect these criteria. They found that subordinates associate different behaviors with leaders who have good relationships with customers and superiors. The research shows that we should be careful about using general effectiveness assessments – several perspectives seem to be valid! This multidisciplinary research produced counterintuitive results.[18]
- Three professors – Ulrich Steger, Paul Strebel and John Ward – specialized in environmental management, strategy and family business, respectively, are working together to research "global corporate governance issues." The backbone of their project was an extensive empirical investigation into different types of corporate governance. Several principal dilemmas of boards were identified, and four distinct clusters of corporate governance were defined.[19] They are now studying evolutionary issues to do with the role of the board in various settings, as well as those regarding joint venture and subsidiary boards.

---

[18] R. Hooijberg and D. Denison, "What makes leaders effective? A stakeholder approach to leadership effectiveness," *IMD Working Paper* (2007).

[19] U. Steger (ed.), *Mastering global corporate governance* (Chichester: Wiley, 2004).

4 Marketing strategy

> Marketing is not the art of finding clever ways to dispose of what you make. It is the art of creating genuine customer value ... Today's smart marketers don't sell products; they sell *benefit packages*. They don't sell *purchase value* only; they sell *use value*.
>
> Philip Kotler[1]

KEY POINTS

- A business school's marketing strategy should be based on assuring take-home value for a learning partner using one or more of the services that the school offers. The value proposition for the various clients cum shareholders must be made clear!
- Relationship marketing with particular firms and individuals is key, based on long-term relationships so the school is able to offer value in terms of a profound understanding of the firm's or individual's needs.
- Marketing of open programs will typically require particularly well-articulated communication. A field sales force of experienced marketing executives (at IMD we call them corporate development directors or CDDs) needs to be in place to ensure that the needs of a particular company are understood, and that there are participants from a diverse range of firms from all over the world attending the school's programs, i.e. to create a "global meeting place."
- The website increasingly represents a critical aspect of the marketing mix. It allows individuals to look for the information that is relevant to them – information on specific programs, the supporting research, testimonials from participants, links to the professors involved and the like.

---

[1] P. Kotler, Kotler Marketing Group, www.kotlermarketing.com/, accessed September 19, 2006.

- Even in the internet age, brochures can still be a useful marketing tool provided they are minimalist – succinct and to the point.
- The use of classical advertising seems rather ineffective when it comes to yielding results in terms of more program enrollment and, therefore, it has a questionable role in the marketing mix – as is the case with most value-creating fields of activity, the advertising space is simply too crowded.
- Word-of-mouth marketing, based on prestige, satisfied customers and a strong image, seems to be more important than ever. Alumni and other networking activities play a key role in this area.

INTRODUCTION

Marketing of value-based services offered by business schools has traditionally involved informing potential customers – through, for example, direct mail campaigns, brochures and the school's website – about the various programs a school has to offer. Often these programs were developed based on a combination of internal perspectives within the school, largely driven by what various professors are able to offer. This "inside-out" approach to program development does not necessarily address the specific needs of learning partners. Today's situation calls for a different approach.

Given the plethora of available programs – including excellent company-run programs, those offered by consulting firms, and so on – the question for business schools is how to stay competitive and not just survive but also excel in the international marketplace. And how do they identify opportunities to do this? To answer these questions, schools that are in the business of developing and delivering executive programs must identify their core competencies – their faculty's skills, knowledge and collective learning about their research areas – to find the school's unique selling propositions. Clearly, there is also a strong need to enter into dialogue with business. The needs of the learning partners must also be taken into account. Building on its core competencies allows a school to resist the temptation to move into areas where it has little or no experience or competence. This means that a school should avoid misrepresenting its capabilities, i.e. it should not respond favorably to learning partner requests when it does not have the competence base to meet them.

In addition to identifying core competencies, business schools, of course, must be able to identify opportunities. Seeing opportunities before they are obvious to everyone else means staying abreast of what is happening in the business environment. A key way to do this is by developing close relationships with the business world. This requires a sizable investment of time in research, knowledge gathering and networking. However, the payoff from this investment can be considerable. Developing a unique and sustainable executive program can have a positive domino effect on the other programs the school offers. Successful bonding with a learning partner in one area can lead to strengthened "renovation" of other activities too!

In this chapter, we shall start by looking at five strategic propositions to guide marketing. We shall then discuss some of the advantages of collaborative relationships when it comes to marketing executive education, and the implications for business schools that focus on relationship marketing. We shall then discuss what a focused portfolio of value-driven services for balanced growth might look like for the modern business school, with particular implications for its marketing strategy. Next, we shall look at marketing in the face of competition and the increasing importance of internet marketing and word-of-mouth referrals. Finally, we will come up with a set of conclusions and implications for business schools.

FIVE SIMPLE STRATEGIC PROPOSITIONS TO GUIDE MARKETING

It is important for a business school to have a few basic strategic paradigms established as the starting point from which it can then develop its specific marketing approach further. In my opinion, five essential paradigms drive business school marketing:

1. *A simple and focused strategy:* Strategy means choice. There are so many different directions that one could potentially follow. A clear focus is key, i.e. to develop a consistent, simple strategy that will enable you to stay on track. Complexity may be the worst enemy of academic value-creation. Academic institutions are simply not good at handling complexity. This can be seen by the relatively narrow set of programs IMD offers – and on one campus! Above all, the executive target group must be very clear.

2. *Everyone must be committed to the strategic direction: Broadly – not singularly:* No academic strategy can take place unless all the people in the organization – clearly the professors but also the staff, including the field force – actually want it to happen. This is because academics – and academic institutions – thrive on excitement; they want to be involved when "fun" things are happening. Therefore, it is essential that the implementation of a strategy follows a path that allows individuals to buy in. A strategy cannot happen if individual faculty members see it as a chore instead of an exciting and fun challenge. Thus, the strategy implementation must create excitement in order to mobilize the energy of the faculty. Not only must an academic institution be a "happy place," but the marketing must also reflect this enthusiasm and excitement, this positive energy. Therefore, there must be broad agreement regarding the basic values. The culture, the brand, the values are key – and the test is why one should believe in this!

3. *Opportunities for faculty initiatives:* It is important that there is room for faculty initiatives, i.e. not everything should be planned to the nth degree, to give some leeway for possible implementation of faculty members' propositions. The feeling that the academic institution is a place that welcomes innovations, initiative and moral thinking is key. Thus, the faculty above all must see new opportunities for academic value-creation before these become obvious to everyone else – the faculty must drive the value-based, self-discovery process discussed in the previous pages. And this –

the faculty's clear commitment to creating new insights and innovations – must be an essential part of the marketing message too!

4. *Effective communication:* In order to communicate the innovative,
   forward-looking vibrancy embedded in the first three paradigms, a
   number of creative communication tools are essential: a strong
   field force; an effective in-company program office; a focused set of
   brochures, accompanied by a targeted database for mailing; and a
   well-developed website. Significantly, the website also strengthens
   the link with alumni – a key source of marketing success. The
   website creates "stickiness." Above all, it is important to be on
   time with the communication – too often, new program initiatives
   fail because of a lack of coordination, which can lead to delays.

5. *A willingness to "invest" in marketing:* A willingness to invest in
   marketing is also critical. For instance, this might now imply more
   resources being spent on web-based marketing. This will allow
   individual executives to more proactively search for specific learning opportunities that they actually would feel that they need –
   rather than having them being unilaterally exposed to traditional
   marketing materials – such as brochures, advertising, etc. Clearly,
   the web must be kept updated. And the flexibility of the search
   function will be key – the web design will typically call for careful
   investments! The traditional marketing materials must of course
   also be updated – the most noticeable trend being "minimalistic"
   marketing – shorter, to-the-point brochures and ads that serve
   more as initial "teasers," to be followed up by "visits on the web,"
   or by the school's marketing field force. The individual learner is
   now much more in command – and the business school must be
   ready to invest to reach these executives.

These five strategic paradigms must be pursued together. This could
result in certain dilemmas, but the dilemmas must be solved in a
positive way. For instance, "strategy means choice" must not be
interpreted to mean that no new initiatives can be pursued, particularly if they are seen as falling "slightly outside" the strategic

direction. It is important that there is enough flexibility to allow for new initiatives while still maintaining focus. The lead and be led value-creation process – where propositional and prescriptive knowledge meet – must provide ongoing vitality to the business school, while still maintaining a sense of simplicity and focus.

COLLABORATIVE *VS.* TRANSACTIONAL RELATIONSHIPS

In order to develop true learning partnerships, business schools must emphasize the importance of building long-term relationships rather than being satisfied with individual transactions. In doing so, they must develop a deeper understanding of their learning partners' needs; only then will they be in a good position to provide relevant programs when required.

It seems important that a business school's marketing activities should properly reflect its commitment to two-way academic value-creation, the lead and be led effect. This calls for the marketing message to be clear: The participants and the companies that sponsor them are not customers, they are learning partners. This means that they must be "sold" the fact that there will be rigorous thought leadership, hard work and the testing of participants' cognitive limits. At the same time, an "open invitation" must be extended to the participants to contribute, to interact and to share their experiences. Clearly, a dynamic two-way, interactive process must be a key theme of the business school's marketing strategy. This means a long-term commitment both ways, a mutual trust, an ability to listen, a commitment to trying to understand the other side, and so on.

Relationship marketing

Gone are the days of the classic "inside-out" approach when the market accepted almost anything coming from a leading business school. Today, a unidirectional "pushing" of "products" no longer works. The marketing activities of the modern business school must focus on relationship marketing. As we have discussed, this requires a much heavier emphasis on being closer to leading corporations, to listening and understanding what is called for in business today. This "outside-in" approach will thus also largely drive the portfolio of programs that the business school offers.

Of course, this market-driven approach must not be taken to extremes. There will always be a need for business schools to lead the development of new thoughts and concepts, as noted, i.e. to drive the market, not only be driven by the market.[2] Above all, research will increasingly be needed to point business in new directions, not only in terms of content but also in terms of pedagogical advances. Still, relationship marketing does imply a clear shift toward a stronger market orientation, with business schools driving development slightly less independently and, instead, being driven more and more by the market and key customer needs.

The question business schools need to explore is how they can decide what type of program offerings are central to this relationship-oriented context. Given that many established professors tend to feel a sense of "ownership" of their unique courses – built up based on their own, often axiomatic research, over a long period of time – it can be particularly difficult to adopt an outside-in approach to program offerings. Many professors may feel that it is their academic right to offer their programs based on an inside-out view. Thus, friction can result when a business school attempts to implement a program port-folio that has a more outside-in approach.

Figure 4.1 gives a view of the portfolio of program propositions offered by a business school such as IMD. As already discussed in Chapter 2, we see that this type of school might offer MBA programs or open-enrollment executive programs, both of which have individual executives as the client, or learning partner. It can also offer Learning Network services and in-company programs, where the partner would typically be the corporation itself. From a marketing point of view, it is important to note that the purchasing decision in this case is made by someone other than the executive who will

[2] N. Kumar, L. Scheer and P. Kotler, "From market driven to market driving," *European Management Journal* 18 (2000), 129.

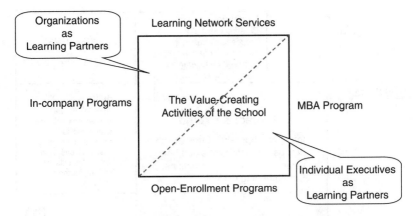

FIGURE 4.1 Conventional marketing challenge seen from IMD's perspective: four types of value-based offerings – balanced to corporations and to individuals.

receive the learning benefits, i.e. someone from corporate human resources or, say, a corporate university function. A clear relationship must thus also be established with key executives in companies to ensure relevance in tailored program offerings. It is also worth pointing out here that although a network of relationships is important, "the products" – i.e. the programs themselves – must be cutting edge. It is the *balance* between strong networks and strong programs that creates stability. Strong relationships alone are not enough!

IMD's revenue-generating activities fall into the four broad areas indicated in Figure 4.1. One offering is open-enrollment programs. This represents approximately 39 per cent of IMD's revenue (including the EMBA Program). Another 41 per cent comes from in-company executive programs. A third offering is IMD's Learning Network, which accounts for 15 per cent of the school's income. Finally, the full-time MBA program represents 5 per cent of IMD's revenue.

VALUE-BASED ACTIVITIES
The value-based activity in a school must start from where the school has established a core of excellence. This starting point – what we call

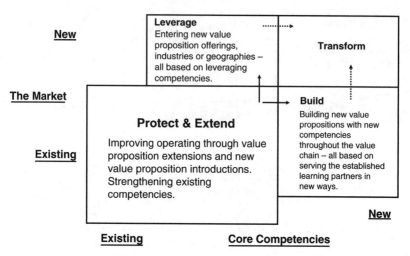

FIGURE 4.2 Basic framework for dynamic value-creation.

Source: B. Chakravarthy and P. Lorange, *Profit or growth? Why you don't have to choose* (Philadelphia, PA: Wharton School Publishing, 2007).

"protect and extend" – would be the foundation of the school's value-based offering. This is illustrated in Figure 4.2.

The two dimensions of this figure are the market and enhancing core competencies. The market dimension requires the ability to see or sense new business opportunities in the marketplace, e.g. new geographies and/or new customers. One example might be to apply a school's core competencies in, say, the marketing area to new segments, such as the service sector or in addressing the low cost competition sector. For example, consider the research led by Adrian Ryans, which is focused on how traditional companies can meet the growing challenge of low cost competitors – competitors who succeed by offering "good enough" products and services at very low prices. Part of this research has focused on developing a deeper understanding of how successful low cost players operate based on the assumption that a deep understanding of competitors is required to develop effective responses. This research has been used as the base for a new program aimed at companies who wish to adopt this strategy to gain competitive advantage.

The second dimension – enhancing core competencies – can be applied to any element of the school's competence base, e.g. strengthened faculty, new research, pedagogical advances, new information technology or new marketing channels. Self-renewal of a school's value base will require the continuous building of new competencies.

It is important to form teams to support specific aspects of strategic growth as outlined in Figure 4.2 – "protect and extend" versus "leverage" versus "build" – perhaps ultimately leading to "transform." Each of these contexts calls for creative thinking based on understanding the customer, and this creative thinking calls for relationships with business. However, the relationship marketing will take on a different flavor in each case.

For "protect and extend," it is a matter of stressing to the existing customer base that current approaches are continuously being renewed – that good can be done even better. Thus, the marketing approach is to stress that the traditional, established programs are still being invested in – still being renewed and extended. For example, the research on low cost competition referred to above has been developed into a new program that will help traditional companies develop strategies and tactics to deal with the low cost competitors that are attacking their businesses. For "leverage," one way would be to take an already proven course offering into a new market, i.e. to find a new customer segment that can be served by a similar type of offering. Another way of developing new offerings would be to add distinctive new competencies to what already works. This would be a "build" strategy.

Both "leverage" and "build" are, of course, only extensions of the initial base of strengths. Having, for instance, developed an extension of an existing offering in a new market, i.e. "leverage," it may then be natural to go one step further and ask what specific additional competence extensions it would make sense to offer as well. In doing so, the business school moves to the "transform" stage, where in the end, both the market and the core competencies would be new. To use the earlier example, if a program was established to help companies develop winning low cost strategies, then clearly new customer segments, such as super-aggressive discount retail chains or others competing on cost such as some airlines or direct financial service companies, might be keen to attend. This of course assumes that they would be willing to spend money on executive development – which might be a heroic assumption! As a logical, related step, specific new competencies would need to be developed so that faculty could effectively deliver classes on how to be an effective low cost provider. Likewise, one can get to "transform" from "protect and extend" via "build."

One must build on one's competencies. And these core competencies must be defined from the clients' point of view. These might be seen as core communities – corporations, professionals, alumni. The core competencies of one's institution must be built to fit these core communities! Perhaps it might also be useful to be explicit about one's core incompetencies in this respect. Strategic choice is key. A school cannot realistically be everything to everyone!

THE MARKETING CHALLENGE FOR NEW VALUE-ADDED SERVICES

We have seen that dynamic value-creation is key for the business school that aspires to serve the rapidly developing corporate market in an effective way. New value-added services need to be marketed, complementing the already established and typically more conventional marketing of existing program services. New markets and/or new core competencies need to be developed to better serve the emerging needs of learning partners. It is important, when adding new core competencies to meet emerging corporate needs, that they are driven by the corporate learning partners, in symbiosis with the faculty's research. Marketing thus takes on an added role as we move from a situation where competencies are in place to one where they need to be added. Both the marketing field force and the in-company programs office serve as important sources of new ideas and foci for the faculty to enhance the lead and be led value-creating process.

The challenge for the school, therefore, is to understand better the mix of marketing messages to be delivered to a particular learning partner – that is, based on a lot of tailoring. Here, too, the field force, the in-company programs office and marketing communications play critical roles. One general trend seems to be clear – increasingly, the company is as much the client as the individual executive. Even for open-enrollment programs, the action-learning agenda applies more often. Frequently, companies send teams of two or more to open programs so that they can discuss the implications of their various new insights and their own strategies when it comes to their companies – and how to implement the necessary changes more effectively. As Julie Harrison, responsible for leadership development training at Allianz Management Institute, notes: "We realize that the impact of sending individuals to executive education and then bringing them back into the organization is like a fish swimming against the current – they have a tough time coming back into the organization. We are finding that sending teams to programs has a powerful impact on the organization when they get back because the team strength is much greater than the individual strength."[3]

The days when individuals were enrolled in open programs as a "reward" or a "pre-retirement gift" are clearly gone! The Learning Network will also be more for the benefit of the firm, rather than of interested individuals. Figure 4.3 illustrates this shift toward marketing to firms in networks (compare with Figure 4.1).

What more can we say? Tailoring, focus and simplicity will be key. The people who are responsible for marketing activities will have to understand that network-driven, value-based marketing is a matter partly of "efforts" for today (protect and extend) and partly of efforts today for tomorrow (build, leverage, transform). And with these various additional value-based initiatives, things can easily become complicated. Effective marketing means being sensitive to cognitive limitations. This means that a workable marketing

---

[3] Büchel and Antunes, "Reflections on executive education."

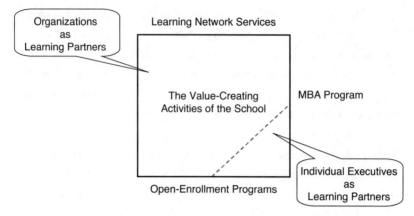

FIGURE 4.3 Marketing challenge: IMD's four types of value-based offerings – balanced in favor of corporations.

strategy must have a set of simple strategic propositions as the basis, along the lines of what we outlined at the beginning of this chapter.

We can see this when it comes to the evolution of IMD's marketing organization. Earlier we referred to the in-company program office. This, in fact, has become a point of synthesis for providing tailored in-company proposals to organizations, often also accompanied by significant input on the subsequent specific tailored program itself. Clearly, this group of accomplished professionals must have both a keen understanding of the more recent overall market trends and a good appreciation of IMD's cutting-edge capabilities, including which professor might be the best one to deliver a particular element of the program. Close networking with the field force of CDDs will be key, particularly during the early proposal development phase. Equally, a close interface with faculty is paramount, when it comes to both the program proposal development and, above all, the program design phase, in which the faculty will typically increasingly take the lead. The in-company program office plays a vital role in networking – with the learning partner, the CDDs and faculty – and in keeping it simple. It needs to reduce complexity, filter out idiosyncratic viewpoints, maintain the focus and come up with a robust essence of what is important for a particular in-company program. Herein lies the key to success.

We can also see this drive toward focusing on the simple essentials when we observe how IMD's program brochures have evolved. Previously, they tended to be rather bulky, with a lot of general messages, supplemented by a large array of pictures, as well as general quotes of support from a random set of executives. Today, by contrast, the brochures are short, to the point and offer clearly tailored marketing messages, with testimonials from practitioners that add clarity.

MARKETING IN THE FACE OF COMPETITION

One could argue that business schools might increasingly have to compete with new entrants in the executive education arena. As touched on earlier, one relatively recent entrant would be consultancies.[4] Another significant potential area of new competition might come from corporate universities.[5] There might even be a tendency now for some corporations to see the selection of executive education programs as a task that belongs to the procurement office. In these cases, there might be a heavy focus on costs – rather than on quality, innovation and freshness of research.

At best, of course, a corporate university could be a great "partner" for a business school, allowing the business school to undertake parts of the research and education mandate of the university. At worst, however, the corporate university could attempt to "cherry pick" professors from business schools and run the programs themselves within the corporate university. They would thus be benefiting from the research that the business school has already paid for to support its faculty. This might indeed be an example of a "free ride!"

---

[4] M. Kipping and C. Amorim, "Consultancies as management schools," in R. P. Amdam, R. Kvalshaugan and E. Larsen (eds.), *Inside the business schools* (Oslo: Abstrakt, 2003).

[5] For the phenomenon of the creation of corporate universities, see S. Crainer and D. Dearlove, *Gravy training: Inside the business of business schools* (San Francisco, CA: Jossey-Bass, 1999), chapter 9.

So what can business schools do in terms of marketing to counter these competitive threats? The key is to emphasize the quality package that the business school can provide: Research, based on effective state-of-the-art concepts *and* strong, pedagogically sound program delivery by the school's own professorial team. And the school's resources back all of this up in order to deliver an integrated, high-quality program underpinned by research and two-way learning in the classroom.

In the end, thus, it will be up to the prospective learning partner to make the various trade-offs – quality versus cost, academic independence versus consultancy, cohesive program delivery from a single team versus piecemeal sessions from independent providers. The marketing team is of course indispensable in articulating these trade-offs, so that the prospective participant can make deliberate, informed choices. One should not ignore the fact that some of the "new" competitive entrants might play down the total quality side, while amplifying some of the assumed benefits of their piecemeal approaches – understandable, but perhaps at times misleading!

ROLE OF THE BRAND

There is no doubt that a strong name, or brand, can be very effective for the marketing of business schools. Harvard Business School, Stanford Graduate School of Business, the Sloan School of Management at MIT, Chicago Graduate School of Business and Dartmouth's Tuck School of Business, to mention a few, come to mind. European-based business schools such as INSEAD and London Business School (LBS) are also good examples of valuable, high-quality business school brands. For all of these, marketing will be facilitated through the strength of their brands!

At IMD, we have been struggling with developing a new brand – IMD – for the past seventeen years! In 1990, two business schools based in the French part of Switzerland – IMI in Geneva and IMEDE in Lausanne – merged. It took a long time to develop a new brand – IMD – a much harder task than anticipated. Why? First of all, the already existing brands – IMI and IMEDE – were well respected. It was hard for the new school to disassociate itself from these two, i.e. difficult to build on them when it came to its new brand. Being a small school, with relatively limited financial means, it was also difficult to undertake an extensive advertising and communication program for the new school and its brand. To be effective, considerable resources would have been required.

To develop a brand based on top-quality focus then became the aim – quite similar in fact to the task of developing luxury brands that can be found in the automotive industry, cosmetics, watches and jewelry and high fashion. A consistent strategy for the development of the IMD brand was thereby developed:

- High quality in all aspects of what IMD is doing – consistency among research, pedagogical delivery, facilities and administrative procedures.
- Limited exposure for the IMD brand – only available at the "global meeting place" in Lausanne. The IMD value proposition cannot be obtained elsewhere.
- Relatively high prices – to signify a high quality value proposition – with no discounting or rebates! The latter is not only critical for the development of the brand, but also an issue of treating all learning partners in a consistent way.

IMD has thus over time been relatively successful in developing a high-quality brand, associated with a relatively small, cutting-edge business school. Consistency around this has been a driver!

Several business schools are attempting to develop consistent brands – to aid them in their marketing, and to be of help in shaping the given school's value proposition. A good example is the Sauder School of Business at the University of British Columbia. Under its dean, Daniel Muzyka, it has developed a brand pyramid, attempting to develop consistency between the "brand essence," the "culture," the "reasons to believe" and the "positioning," as can be seen in Figure 4.4.

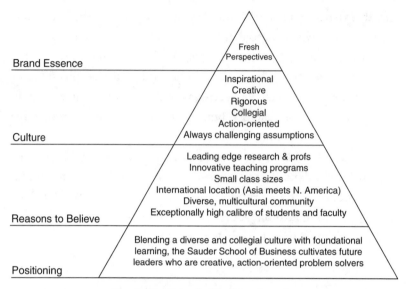

FIGURE 4.4 The Sauder School of Business brand pyramid.

Source: D. Muzyka, Dean, Sauder School of Business, University of British Columbia – private correspondence, 2007.

INTERNET MARKETING

There is no doubt that the need for clear, honest communication of a school's value proposition is becoming more important than ever for the effective marketing of a business school. As there is a wealth of "information" available at the click of a mouse to anyone with a computer and an internet connection, this medium has assumed a critically important role in marketing, particularly as people need to know which information – which websites – they can trust to be relevant and reliable.

Any business school worthy of the name now has to have a top notch, comprehensive website if it wants to stay in the game. This allows the school to present all its program offerings, along with clear messages about the benefits of each and who might attend. It can also provide all the necessary administrative tools, such as brochures, application forms and quick contact with the school, as well as appropriate tracking tools to ensure the website is achieving its objective and meeting evolving customer needs. Other instant information available on the website includes faculty member profiles, highlighting their current research interests and projects. Testimonials and forums for sharing experiences and knowledge are other components of a typical business school website.

What matters, above all, is that prospective learning partners can look at what they as individuals see as relevant, without being inundated with marketing messages *per se*. A well-designed website should allow them to find the support they need to meet their specific development needs, as well as keep them informed about current cutting-edge topics. At IMD, we present these topics as "Tomorrow's Challenges" (also discussed in Chapter 3 as a means of rapidly disseminating some of IMD's key research insights). Visitors to the "Tomorrow's Challenges" page on the website can choose a topic that interests them and then read and rate it – and even download it if they wish. There is an interactive element here, which – apart from promoting knowledge sharing – is useful from a marketing research perspective. The ratings of articles and any comments are passed on to the relevant people, for example the author. A graphic device shows at a glance how popular individual articles are – the bigger the box, the more readers – and how recent, with a more vivid color indicating the newer articles. All this feedback provides valuable insights into what the most popular topics currently are and pointers for us to consider when developing new programs.

Prospective learning partners will hopefully continue to visit the website for updates and actively *want* to attend a program (as opposed to being sent on one by the HR department). And alumni will be able to stay in touch and find out about relevant developments and may *want* to come back or may refer programs to colleagues based on their experience at IMD. This indeed is "sticky" marketing. One more example to illustrate this is the MBA diary, which has between 600 and 700 subscribers in any given year. A number of MBAs have noted that it played an influential role in their choice of IMD as a business school. About 65 per cent of the subscribers to the MBA diary tend to result in applications to the MBA program. During the application process, it allowed them to find out more about what to expect; once they are here, it provides their family and friends with details of what they are doing, especially as they do not often have the time to call or write!

Needless to say, an effective website requires heavy institutional investment – not only in funds for the software and technical development but also, and perhaps more significantly, in time for preparing and updating the multitude of materials that are featured on the site. There are thus two critical success factors: Keep the website minimalist, focused on the essentials that the school can offer, and avoid the temptation to overload it with extensive, often peripheral, items; and keep it up to date – it *must* be fresh!

The internet, of course, is also playing an increasingly important role pedagogically in its own right, and some may see this as competition for business schools. I do not see it this way, however. As already mentioned, IMD's weekly webcast enjoys a great deal of success and *complements* the executive learning taking place on campus. But I am relatively skeptical about internet-based executive education becoming a freestanding activity because the "global meeting place" aspect is lost.[6] One exception, perhaps, might be when it comes to covering the very basic, preparatory aspects of executive development. For instance, in IMD's Building on Talent program, the participants are expected to cover basic accounting, finance and management skills via internet-based educational modules before they arrive at IMD. Overall, though, I do not expect the internet to offer an alternative to top-level executive education. Rather, the internet offers great ways to complement a business school's main lines of academic offerings. As I see it, the key role of the internet for a business school is definitely in marketing the school.

---

[6] For the development of executive education over the internet, see P. J. van Baalen and L. T. Moratis, *Management education in the network economy: Its context, content, and organization* (Dordrecht: Kluwer, 2001).

WORD OF MOUTH

Word-of-mouth referrals are a vital factor in the success of any business school's programs. And the best way to foster these referrals is by keeping the school's learning partners happy and by developing meaningful, value-added opportunities for networking and lifelong learning so that the top-of-mind awareness is preserved – crucial for word-of-mouth referrals to happen spontaneously. So how can a business school maintain ownership of the space between the ears of its learning partners so that it is top of mind when they, their companies or their colleagues have particular executive development needs? As we have emphasized throughout this book, designing and delivering quality programs based on cross-disciplinary research that is truly beneficial to the learning partners attending them is, of course, fundamental if learning partners are going to walk away with their expectations having been met or, better yet, exceeded. The next step is to create ways to maintain relationships with these learning partners – now alumni – both individuals and companies.

Ultimately, a school's access to resources and a school's likelihood of long-term survival will have a lot to do with its reputation and with the quality of its alumni base. The performance of IMD's alumni is generally strong. Many have achieved leading positions in their careers. IMD's reputation, in general, has also strengthened over the last fifteen years.

As we have discussed, IMD has a Learning Network in place that advances our relationships with our corporate learning partners through networking and lifelong learning activities. We also have an Alumni Network, with more than 55,000 members around the world. The IMD Alumni Network offers a range of networking and ongoing learning events for learning partners following their program experiences on campus. The benefits for alumni include:

- *IMD alumni clubs:* The forty alumni clubs offer an annual agenda of planned speaking events and social activities, which serve to bring alumni together in their region – and worldwide. As well as providing networking opportunities, they serve to extend the IMD learning experience beyond its programs.

- *Events:* Every two years, IMD holds a major alumni weekend get-together at our Lausanne campus. The entire event is organized to provide a stimulating learning and networking environment. This event has covered a range of topics such as current trends in global competition and the role of the next generation of the internet. IMD also organizes special events for the further development of its alumni, ranging from international conferences on business management themes to local events that bring together alumni from a certain country or region.
- *Class reunions:* IMD's Alumni Network office will work with alumni to plan and provide support for their class reunions on campus – again providing excellent opportunities for renewing friendships, networking and learning.
- *Information Center:* A major benefit for alumni is that they can ask the Information Center to carry out research for them. Alumni are also welcome to visit the campus to use the Information Center facilities, including the online databases and more than 350 periodicals.
- *Alumni directory:* IMD alumni have exclusive access to this directory, which can prove useful for keeping in touch with other alumni. This directory is, of course, online.
- The benefits for IMD – another virtuous cycle where alumni's top-of-mind awareness results in more referrals. More referrals mean more learning partners and more learning partners mean more alumni. And the cycle continues. . .

IMPLICATIONS FOR BUSINESS SCHOOLS

The marketing activities in a business school today are very different from those that existed a few years ago. With the modern knowledge society, and with the need for business schools to develop close

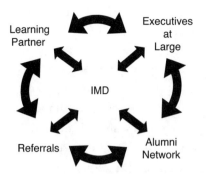

FIGURE 4.5 Virtuous cycle of word-of-mouth referrals

relationships with their learning partners, the emphasis will increasingly be on market-driven outside-in relationship marketing, as opposed to the more traditional inside-out program-specific marketing. The question is, how can this take place?

It requires business schools to *listen* to their learning partners, both inside and outside the classroom, and to be catalysts for new academic insights, along the lines we have discussed. It also calls for a reorganization of the inner workings of the business school to eliminate structural impediments that only serve to foster "preservation of the status quo," internal politics and a lack of speed. And, of course, it calls for a marketing strategy that can meaningfully convey this message when it comes to brochures, value pricing, databases, the behavior of the sales force and now also the website. Effective marketing, indeed commercial success for the school, rests on:

1. *Building on core competencies:* Achieving balanced growth while also emphasizing the present areas of strength will have implications for the marketing strategy of a business school. This needs to be carefully worked out by building on the "protect and extend" activities that truly work. This must be complemented with the development of new markets and the introduction of new knowledge, building on established strengths – in terms of content and/or network. All in all, marketing of the new developments – the fresh thinking, the dynamism – as part

of the business school's value-creation is now more central than ever.

2. *Positioning and value-based pricing:* Research-based executive programs – compared with the many that are *de facto* not based on current research and thought leadership – are not commodities and should not be positioned as such. They should, instead, be positioned as high value-added services for learning partners – as prestige products – and priced based on the value (return on investment) that the learning partners perceive they will realize from the programs. This goes far beyond offering a particular program to a particular executive, where cost considerations may be more of a driver. It is enhanced value, not costs, that must drive the marketing.

3. *Marketing communications:* In the past, freestanding programs were typically sold based on a business school's reputation. However, in the increasingly competitive business of executive development, the modern business school will need to develop new marketing communication tools – tools that express the school's commitment to two-way academic value-creation and its prestige positioning. All marketing communications, such as brochures and the website, must reflect this "Rolex quality," as well as the learning partner's perceived value, i.e. what are the take-home benefits? The marketing communications materials should reflect the expectations of the customer rather than focus on the virtues of the school, and they should be minimalist, providing crisp, tailored messages that specifically communicate, "*Why* this program is for me!"

4. *Key account management:* There is a clear key account management challenge today. It is important to gain a much better understanding of how relationships develop and evolve with particular companies. The pattern of the relationship for a given firm must be entirely clear – across various program offerings, various geographies and for various organizational entities. Sophisticated databases, such as Siebel, are becoming more and

more critical in managing these relationships. And the relationships should be developed with many executives in the corporation – the alumni, the divisional human resources functions and senior management, not just with the corporate human resources function. It is vital that no single person or small group of people – either on the learning partner side or within the business school's own organization – should be allowed to monopolize a relationship. It is for all and should not be hijacked! One should never lose sight of the fact that all key accounts, all relationships must in the end rest on top quality programs, based on cutting-edge thought leadership and research, and the relationship must be broadly based.

5. *Highly qualified field force:* To manage relationships with learning partners successfully, a highly competent, specialized field force will be necessary. Effective marketing will thus be heavily based on personal, face-to-face relationships. More conventional sales techniques, such as those that rely on advertising and/or brochures, will no longer suffice. Instead, the field force must work with specific companies on a systematic basis, attempting to develop a "partnership" with each given company. They must focus on supporting learning partners and building relationships with them. The "client" must see the field force representative as an asset, i.e. someone who can play the role of educational consultant and be able to advise and suggest programs – open enrollment or in-company – based on a deep understanding of the company's particular needs. It is critical that the field force no longer pushes every program offering to everyone; instead, they must be a catalyst in helping to find the right program for the particular situation. The key is *tailoring:* Relationship selling is *in;* hard product selling is out!

6. *An effective website:* This is becoming increasingly critical. Above all, it allows individuals to access the business school over the internet, from their home or office or virtually anywhere, when they want pertinent information – truly an outside-in way

of communicating. A lot of information regarding specific programs, research activities, alumni news and other potentially interesting events can be put on the website. An effective, well-designed website can be a major driver for marketing – and we can anticipate that it will become even more important in the future. And this is logical; the website allows individuals to access what interests *them* in terms of relevant thought leadership and programs, i.e. they can tailor the information to their needs and are not constantly bombarded with information they do not want at inconvenient times. It is outside-in marketing at its best!

7. *Alumni – and word-of-mouth:* Nothing is more powerful than "happy customers." Thus, it is important to maintain an active relationship with them – the alumni. Satisfied alumni may often turn into repeat customers, that is, as participants of another program. Or, in the case of IMD's Orchestrating Winning Performance (OWP) program, which essentially has "new" content every year, alumni may come back to this very program again and again, for a new "vitamin injection." For instance, during the ten-year history of OWP, 180 participants have come back two or more times, with some coming back as many as six times!

Alumni, of course, may also be great proponents for programs by referring them to colleagues and friends – hopefully based on a genuinely positive experience and enthusiasm. While it is difficult to substantiate what percentage of participants come from alumni referrals, our anecdotal evidence suggests that more than half are influenced by alumni.

It follows from this that relationships with alumni must be kept strong – and vibrant! The school's website, support provided to the alumni clubs and reunions, etc., are key. Perhaps even more effective are specific follow-on mailings of relevant, substantive materials to participants who have attended specific programs.

IMD's marketing model

IMD's portfolio of activities includes open-enrollment programs, in-company programs, the MBA programs and the Learning Network. The open-enrollment programs are promoted via IMD's corporate development directors or CDDs (a sales force of twelve senior specialists, with MBA-type qualifications, who act as network partners with each learning partner company, as well as with specific individuals). This team covers the whole world.

The in-company programs are marketed by an in-company program office at IMD, which responds to requests from corporations. The requests can be the result of contacts with individual faculty members, they can come via CDDs, they can be the result of repeat business or they can be initiated by an individual company that wishes to tap into IMD's capabilities. Reputation is key here. Tailored proposals are then written, which lead to a go/no go decision from the company.

The Learning Network is marketed in much the same way as in-company programs. To some extent, companies join the network because they are required to be members in order to be offered a tailored in-company program. Companies that participate in such programs *must* be considered long-term learning partners, hence this link. However, it is exciting to see that the network is now becoming a "commercial product" in its own right, with many companies joining in order to benefit from the Wednesday Webcasts and the Discovery Events as freestanding learning inputs. Clearly, IMD does not see it as a primary task to market this service actively, *per se*, since it might be seen as representing competition with what IMD offers. But, *de facto*, it is indeed a unique vehicle for relationship marketing! Good corporate relationships are formed, which can lead to future business.

The MBA program is marketed through a dedicated MBA office, which makes use of attendance at MBA recruitment fairs, the website, brochures and the like. Through word of mouth, the alumni also serve as strong generators of candidates. And many alumni attend the recruitment fairs to give feedback that is more personal to prospective candidates about what the IMD MBA is *really* like. The program's excellent reputation is key (see Appendix I for rankings). The CDDs also market the MBA program when there is an opportunity, although this is not their main priority. Above all, however, it is the prestige of the MBA program – elite, small, world class and global that facilitates the marketing.

A note of clarification is needed regarding the marketing of the Executive MBA (EMBA) program, as this differs from the marketing of the MBA program. As noted, the first 10 weeks (5 plus 5) of the EMBA program are in fact the Program for Executive Development (PED). In addition, the EMBA program will require another 7.5 weeks of classroom work, plus project work and exercises, virtually monitored. The marketing of the school's PED program is key to the success of the EMBA program and this is done through IMD's field force (CDDs), as well as via mailings and web-based marketing. The candidates are only admitted to the EMBA program after having completed the PED program – and IMD's faculty will typically have a rather realistic view regarding the qualifications of each applicant by then. Out of approximately 240 PED candidates yearly, about one quarter continue with the EMBA program, i.e. approximately 60 per year.

The Alumni Network is also marketed! A web portal has been specifically designed for communicating the activities of the forty alumni clubs, and IMD professors and leading executives are typically featured at alumni gatherings around the world. The considerable investment in the web to allow better linkages with alumni can, of course, also be seen as an important part of IMD's marketing activities.

Every year, the alumni club presidents are invited to IMD for two days of discussion on how the school – and its program – can be positioned better, how alumni activities that the school is involved in can be structured and how the alumni clubs can learn more from each other – "best practice marketing"!

5   Institutional learning

in situations of rapid change only those that are flexible, adaptive and productive will excel. For this to happen, it is argued, organizations need to discover how to tap people's commitment and capacity to learn at *all* levels.

Peter Senge[1]

KEY POINTS

- It is the aggregate of learning from all learning partnerships, from all executive programs, from all research, from all other interactions with learning partners that constitutes the institutional learning for a business school. Process development is part of this!
- Choice is essential in terms of learning partners, teaching programs and rewards so that meaningful institutional learning can take place within selected areas of knowledge, consistent with the school's chosen strategy.
- Increasingly, it may be difficult to distinguish between the institutional learning that goes on in a business school and the institutional learning that goes on in the learning partner organization. Both entities are change partners and, therefore, learning partners in making the organizations' strategies work better.
- An open-minded, "we, we, we" attitude from all is necessary so that effective learning can in fact take place – as opposed to an individualistic, "me, me, me" culture, which would make institutional learning more difficult.

INTRODUCTION

As businesses face new challenges, so, therefore, do business schools – hence the need for business schools to be learning organizations too.

---

[1] P. Senge, *The fifth discipline: The art and practice of the learning organization* (New York: Doubleday, 1990).

Change is the impetus for learning – it is an ongoing and creative process. It starts with understanding the competencies residing within the school and knowing how they can be enhanced and put to use. These competencies can exist at both the individual and the collective level – the total competence of the school depends on the competence of the individual members and the ability of the school to mobilize the individuals to continually increase their capacity to produce results they really care about. At the center of this is, as we have said before, research-based teaching – the lead and be led effect that can take place when propositional knowledge from research meets prescriptive knowledge from the best of practice. Individuals, teams, even the entire institution, learn this way.

In this chapter, we will discuss how change drives institutional learning, as well as the different kinds of institutional learning and how to operationalize them in a business school. We will also discuss how a focus on learning partner companies can be valuable to institutional learning and note the importance of choosing a clear destiny and developing a comprehensive strategy that encourages institutional learning and creates value.

CHANGE DRIVES LEARNING

As a result of the rapid changes taking place in the business environment, companies are increasingly concluding that perhaps the last remaining source of competitive advantage can be found only in investing in improving the people in the organization. This has led to strong pressure for business schools – particularly those that focus on executive development – to change in order to face up to this challenge. Driven by the fact that the critical factors in their environments are changing at a dramatic rate, both individual faculty members and business schools have largely concluded that they must become more effective learners and learning organizations if they are to remain competitive.

Research, program development and program delivery must of course all reflect this rapidly changing agenda. Additionally, it is essential that business schools and their faculty master new types of learning methodologies (e.g. distance learning), as executives will now have a growing need to learn on the job, i.e. ongoing lifelong learning. Since most of the drivers for change will come from business, it is becoming even more critical for business schools to be able to attract classes of top-notch executives from all over the world. The prescriptive knowledge coming from the practitioners is becoming even more important, relatively speaking. The faculty must be able to listen more and better! All of this means more change for business schools, as they strive to become more effective learning organizations.

For a business school to become a learning organization, there are three complementary types of learning it can pursue – or at least informally allow:

1. Individual learning, driven by an individual faculty member's research and the lead and be led effect, which results in accumulated learning.
2. Teams of faculty learning together through research and by teaching their research propositions in programs.
3. Individual faculty as well as faculty teams learning with the business school's corporate learning partners, based on the accumulated learning effects from such learning partnerships.

THE FACULTY MEMBER AS LEARNER

At the individual faculty member level, a great deal of learning has traditionally taken place, especially in order to stay abreast of the advances in each one's – typically disciplinary or axiomatic – field. Individual learning, often based on traditional modes of scientific discovery and involving classical research designs such as hypothesis testing, is at the heart of most faculty members' concerns. Individual, research-based learning of this type, however, is too often one-way, rather than being built on a two-part exchange.

Also, there can often be a multitude of demands on the time of individual faculty members – intensive teaching loads, endless meetings, compliance with excessive bureaucracy and the like. All of this takes away valuable research time, and sometimes the inclination to do research and to learn – precisely because of the lack of time – which leads to a vicious circle. As a result, institutional learning also suffers.

Another factor that may inhibit meaningful individual learning is the promotion and tenure process found typically in academia. Young academics may tend to work on established "safe" research items in order to achieve success in their disciplinary fields, but this might limit their relevant, real-world learning. And, as discussed earlier, this process can often discourage eclecticism, experimentation and, therefore, innovation. Furthermore, professors with tenure might be tempted to slow down and not stay up to speed in their fields. Conservative, ivory tower behavior often results. The hierarchical nature of most business schools, with different roles and privileges at the full professor level versus the associate and assistant professor levels, might further slow down balanced individual faculty learning. And external activities, such as outside consulting, may also interfere with the individual faculty member's learning.

Individuals, therefore, often do not have the time to develop an academic value-based activity agenda that might better reflect the needs of today's environment. Since change and learning go hand in hand, it is understood that a rigid, discipline-based academic culture, perhaps coupled with a highly formalized and politicized inflexible institutional structure, does not necessarily foster a strong learning focus. Instead, it is probably important that the academic institution encourage "curiosity" and "enthusiasm around research." In the best-case scenario, this can lead to peer pressure on all to be involved – as active researchers and active learners.

Despite all of this, there are many ways for individual faculty members to learn from their teaching activities, their research and their outside consulting. Individual learning in academia is, after all, a highly personal matter. It does, however, require individual determination – the discipline and commitment of each faculty member to continue to learn and develop as an individual. The various forces that get in the way often lead to difficult trade-offs and dilemmas, which can be resolved only if each faculty member takes responsibility for his or her ongoing learning agenda.

The academic institution, of course, can help support faculty members in their efforts to maintain their effective learning agendas, say, through annual planning meetings where faculty members' research and pedagogical progress are reviewed. Still, it is only through the faculty member's own self-referencing that fundamental individual learning can take place. This individual learning will also be the backbone for all forms of institutional learning because it results in an organizational accumulation of learning.

What more can the academic institution do? As noted, it is important that the academic institution gives the faculty member time and peace to do research – few committees, little bureaucracy, no academic departments. And the institution must give the professor encouragement – through review meetings to assess the progress of research as well as through meaningful bonuses. Finally, the academic institution must provide resources that support research, e.g. ensuring that research associates, funds and sabbaticals are made available as appropriate.

DISCIPLINE-BASED INSTITUTIONAL LEARNING

Institutional learning or organizational learning, of course, implies that more than one person is involved, that there is a common body of learning, which exists beyond the accumulation of purely individual learning. Traditionally, as pointed out, the value-creating activities in business schools tend to be focused on academic disciplines. This format might lend itself to institutional learning around a discipline-based cluster of colleagues with similar academic backgrounds. There might be a group of marketing professors, for instance, who to a greater or lesser extent, collaborate on certain marketing-related research projects. Typically, the members of this group might also be asked to offer the various marketing-related academic courses or modules in the teaching curriculum. The same applies to faculty groups in other disciplinary fields, such as finance, accounting, operational management and the like.

Learning based on clusters of professors within the same discipline can be seen as attractive from the point of view of individual faculty members, as they can link up with their colleagues around a particular discipline and continue to evolve their own individual discipline-based area of interest. Since "the rules of the game" for this type of research and teaching are well established and have been dictated by what makes sense for advancing knowledge in the given discipline, this can be highly time-efficient for the faculty member. One positive effect of this might be an increased ability to publish axiomatic articles, particularly since most leading academic journals tend to be discipline-based.

The downside of discipline-based institutional learning, however, might be that it leads to a certain narrowness in the institutional learning that takes place. In particular, it can be difficult to find the right balance between real-world learning and narrower, often abstract, disciplinary learning. Because executives do not necessarily think and act in terms of disciplines such as marketing, manufacturing and finance, for example, the faculty member who operates in a strongly fragmented, discipline-based environment may miss some of the change signals that are coming from real-world business. This can result in unrealistic institutional learning. It is the inside-out implication of this type of research-based value-creation that creates the biggest friction with the reality-driven needs of the rapidly changing business environment today. This changing environment calls for an outside-in approach – more ability to listen, typically more eclecticism and a realization that the prescriptive knowledge from good practice is becoming relatively more important.

For all types of institutional learning, it is thus important that the faculty members be connected in more eclectic clusters, that they have open minds, and that they have the will to share an understanding regarding the common knowledge within this cluster. Only through such shared understanding will the necessary institutional learning be meaningful, and manifest itself in institutional action such as better programs, better research output and the like. Faculty members who keep their research findings and learning insights "under wraps," motivated by fear that others might steal their work, while unfortunately not uncommon, is the very antithesis of institutional academic learning.

FOCUS ON LEARNING PARTNERS FOR INSTITUTIONAL LEARNING

Today, with perhaps more openness regarding the ways in which academic value might be created within a business school, there seems to be, as we have noted, an increasing desire to tip the balance toward more practical, relevance-driven institutional learning. This inevitably calls for a different type of approach from business schools that focus on executive education. So, what changes does a business school need to implement to allow it to develop its institutional learning so that it can become a true learning partner with leading companies?

The answer probably lies primarily in identifying and developing relationships with firms from which business schools can truly learn. These powerful, state-of-the-art companies are typically leading multinationals that are generally able to articulate advanced prescriptive knowledge based on the way they conduct their business. Through strong learning partnerships with these companies, faculty can perhaps be encouraged and stimulated to enter into a lead and be led process, where the professors bring their propositional knowledge to the table in exchange for prescriptive, practical knowledge from the companies. Hence, we see the importance of more full-blown learning partnerships between business schools and leading firms as learning organizations to create new knowledge that is research based.

In Figure 5.1, we present a model for conceptualizing the learning partner companies of a business school as learning organizations in learning partnerships with the school. The "menu" for learning in

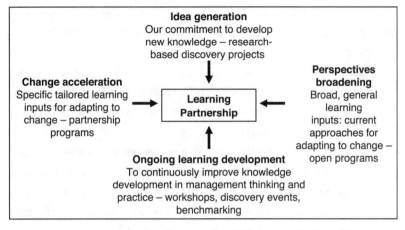

FIGURE 5.1 A menu of organizational learning at a learning partner company.

Source: Adapted from P. Lorange, *New vision for management education: Leadership challenges* (Oxford: Elsevier, 2002).

Figure 5.1 will have to be determined by the specific context and based on the strategic agenda of the company in question. An important aspect of this is that learning is not synonymous with course-based, acquisitional knowledge only. This approach implies that learning can probably best take place when we have a multifaceted interface with learning partner companies, a more open-minded search for new knowledge based on stimulating the curiosity and desire of members of the organization to continuously improve (see the vertical arrows in Figure 5.1).

Interactive, cooperative research efforts between business school faculty and the learning partner company could play an important role here. Another useful way to generate openness to learning and respect for new knowledge is workshops where the implications for various companies from research findings are presented and discussed. Again, this offers another opportunity to achieve lead and be led value-creation. These discovery events (as we refer to them at IMD) will not only expose executives from the learning partner companies to new research but will also allow for benchmarking in terms of how different companies internalize the research findings, i.e. how different firms might modify their prescriptive knowledge as a result of this academic value-generating process.

The course-based learning activities are captured by the horizontal arrows in Figure 5.1. These might consist partly of open-enrollment programs, chosen based on their ability to support the general strategic agenda of the learning partner in question, and partly of in-company programs that might more directly support the company's strategic agenda. All programs can probably be most effective if teams of executives attend, so that the learning is more broadly anchored in the organization, rather than being invested in solo individuals who can easily be ignored by the rest of the organization when they come back with their personal experiences.

The key is for an organization to be able to allow its prescriptive knowledge – "how we do business" – to be modified based on the new insights gained. Typically, this can be more easily achieved when several executives jointly reach the conclusion that some specific change (in the prescriptive way) is required. Such a team might then have a better chance of achieving follow-through "back home." A positive aspect of learning in open programs is, of course, that one learns a great deal from executives from other organizations and from all over the world, i.e. a complement to in-company program learning where the focus is more targeted, perhaps even more inward-looking.

For the business school as a learning organization, it will be important to try to develop a deliberate set of learning partner relationships, so that the aggregate pattern of learning for the business school is also meaningful. Figure 5.2 is an attempt to draw a picture of such an aggregate pattern based on a number of learning partner relationships with individual companies. Several important questions arise from this.

The types of research activities undertaken with the various learning partners will largely drive the overall pattern of research in this type of business school-cum-learning organization. The aim

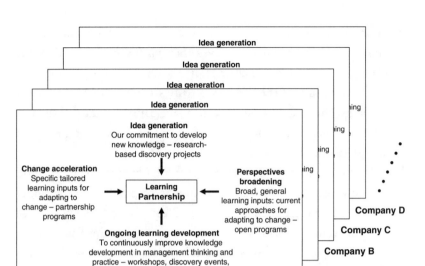

FIGURE 5.2 An aggregated pattern of learning partnerships.

Source: Adapted from P. Lorange, *New vision for management education: Leadership challenges* (Oxford: Elsevier, 2002).

would be for the aggregate picture to provide some sort of higher order and rationale, so that the various research interactions with each learning partner company can lead to an overall logic in the way that knowledge is being developed in the business school as a whole. The interplay between propositional knowledge and prescriptive knowledge must have some degree of similarity over several firms – i.e. not be totally disjointed. It is, of course, therefore critical to try to influence the choice of learning partner companies in such a way that an overall research logic does indeed develop.

This could manifest itself in terms of clusters of faculty with expertise in important areas of joint interest to several learning partner companies. As an example, take the work at IMD in doing research and delivering executive programs on "the finance function" with leading firms. This entails bringing forward thought leadership propositions by the faculty on topics such as key issue-oriented controls, gaining leadership inputs on strategies by members of the finance staff of the various companies, emphasizing the importance of a non-bureaucratic style, and the like. In each of the leading firms we are working with, the executives then put forward how they see good finance and control practices, and good prescriptive knowledge. For IMD, the result of this process is truly strengthened institutional knowledge. This improved organizational learning focus will thus be based on the aggregate effects from the research dimension across a set of key learning partner companies.

It is clear that the overall capacity of a business school could become a limiting factor when it comes to responding to the aggregated pattern of learning partnerships. Clearly, there may be faculty constraint issues. It seems important when up against these constraints to respond in a flexible way to learning partner expectations, making trade-offs where necessary, in order to allocate scarce faculty resources from an overall school perspective. It seems critical that individual faculty members do not make isolated allocation decisions when the school has capacity constraints. Instead, these decisions should be made from an overall school-wide portfolio viewpoint.

In practice, many business schools have taken on relationships with companies based on their teaching needs as the key driver. Learning from the collaborative research side has often been seen as incidental, or has even been neglected altogether. The problem is, that if the clustering of research interests and knowledge build-up is not considered as part of the choice of specific learning partner relationships, it is difficult to develop a meaningful accumulation of research-based knowledge. Above all, a research-based institutional learning dimension will have the real potential to lend a sharper, cutting-edge focus to the business school. The lack of a deliberate institutional learning focus is likely to lead to disjointed institutional learning for the business school – it may, at worst, be pulled apart by the diverse inputs from its learning partners, rather than being pulled together!

The aggregated learning partner model, therefore, should ideally lead to four complementary organizational learning points at the business school, with perhaps the main driver for choosing learning partner companies being the research dimension:

1. *Research activities:* The research activities would be based on what the chosen firms are most interested in, matched of course with the research issues in which the faculty are interested – typically a cluster of faculty with similar research interests. There should be an interest in a certain area of propositional knowledge from the faculty point of view, which would ideally enhance thought leadership from the firms' point of view. The firms must thus also find this particular set of propositions interesting. Needless to say, there will have to be openness among the faculty, leading to dialogue with key learning partner companies on various research options, which might lead to an adjustment regarding what makes sense for research topics, from both the faculty and the learning partner. In the end, an institutional learning effect can be created at both the business school and the learning partner organization – a lead and be led process!

   While research, of course, will always be driven by the faculty's own interests – and this is the way it must be in order to do good research – the academic institution can take certain steps to improve coordination around some propositional knowledge areas. The informal location of faculty offices, for instance, can be important; grouping them along disciplinary lines may be less productive. Information exchange, i.e. broader awareness among faculty members of the types of research others are doing, can also be useful, and this is where a research coordination office can play a role. Faculty research reviews can also give rise to more coordination.

   Parallel consideration must also be given to a prospective partner firm's interest in contributing to the other three learning points.
2. *Discovery events:* Ideally, the research will lead to the organization of various types of discovery events, where the participating

companies can get together and learn from one another as they consider the research that has been generated. At this point, the task will be to develop meaningful patterns of knowledge to focus on so that it can be discussed and expanded with the learning partners, based on joint interests. This is where propositional knowledge meets prescriptive knowledge.

3. *Portfolio of open-enrollment programs:* Often, teaching programs tend to be offered according to tradition, individual faculty initiatives, trends and expectations of "normal" business school offerings. From the perspective of a learning partner relationship, the question should be: What types of open programs would best address the needs of a given learning partner? Of course, many learning partner firms will have relatively similar needs. The open-enrollment program portfolio would thus be structured according to what the companies need, probably being more heavily focused on state-of-the art general management programs where it might be particularly beneficial to interact with other firms. For the institutional learning of the school, the key benefit is to bring relevant, cutting-edge prescriptive knowledge to bear, articulated by the participants.

4. *In-company programs:* Obviously, by their very nature, it is important for each in-company program to reflect the specific strategic needs of the individual learning partners but, at the same time, an in-company program should build up the institutional learning of both the business school and the company. It is hoped that the learning partner may be facing sufficiently interesting challenges to generate true learning insights so that a meaningful lead and be led process results!

All in all, there seems to be an entirely different activity pattern for academic value-creation in business schools that are driven by learning partnerships. The choice of research, based on what the leading companies truly need, is disseminated via vehicles that are accessible to managers, such as discovery events. This would be coupled with a set of general management open-enrollment programs that would be renewed on a continual basis, based on the knowledge stemming from the ongoing research. Finally, this would also be coupled with in-company programs tailored to specific learning partner organizations to accelerate their given strategies, again based on heavy input from the research side. But the underlying academic value-creation process remains fundamentally the same, based on the interplay between propositional and prescriptive knowledge – in various forms, forums and ways, as we have seen! All of this would hopefully lead to the accumulation of clusters of knowledge not only along all four dimensions of focus but also, in the end, within the faculty as a whole, i.e. true institutional learning!

PROCESS DEVELOPMENT AS INSTITUTIONAL LEARNING

Institutional process learning is also key. For instance, the process of providing faculty incentives, reviewing faculty plans and providing feedback is one that can become more efficient over time, due to learning. This might have to do with developing a more appropriate format for plans, for establishing an experience regarding how faculty reviews can be improved – with a focus on key issues, for developing a clearer way to give feedback, and for each faculty member to understand better what this means.

Processes are a key element in "making good even better." And learning is critical so that processes can be executed better. But bureaucratization must be avoided! Processes should not stifle! They should be minimalistic. This might be particularly key for control and human-resource-related processes. Institutional learning should facilitate simplification to achieve minimalism – not add complexity and bureaucracy!

IMPLICATIONS FOR BUSINESS SCHOOLS

Institutional learning will be a key driver for any leading business school that wants to advance and respond to the challenges of its learning partners. Speed, dynamism and change are the order of the day. These issues are great for any leading business school. They become particularly significant, perhaps, when the change agenda is reconciled with the change agendas of learning partner companies; hence, the need for the business school to see itself as a learning organization in order to create inner order and focus and not be blown away by "centrifugal" forces! Following are some of the key implications for business schools:

1. *Adopt a learning partnership focus:* The traditional organizational change agenda with its discipline-based focus might lead to institutional learning that is "skewed" and not effective enough to support properly a realistic, partner-based evolution of the business school's strategy. This can be avoided, in part, by involving clusters of faculty members in meaningful, practitioner-oriented, real-world-driven research and/or teaching programs, thus exposing the faculty as teams or clusters more directly to the learning requirements of living organizations.

   Institutional learning can be further strengthened by developing a closer, holistic link between learning partner organizations and the business school, including joint work on research, workshops based on research, benchmarking, in-company learning activities and even involvement in open-enrollment program activities. In my opinion, the change agenda works both ways and, thus, the learning agenda of the business school as well as of the specific firm can benefit greatly from this learning partnership focus.

2. *Create an environment for institutional learning:* This strategy requires a keen sense of choice – a faculty group can probably work effectively with only a relatively small number of leading learning partner companies, doing more with fewer learning partners. This calls for a deliberate organizational culture in the business school that allows for this type of institutional learning to occur, without being unduly "derailed" by opportunistic pressures from *ad hoc* requests for programs or research from random firms and organizations. But it requires discipline to be able to say "no!" Developing

a faculty culture that achieves this is particularly rewarding, since faculty who largely adopt this approach can expect to see the benefits of institutional learning, the accumulation of thought leadership and cutting-edge propositional knowledge in a forceful way.

3. *Understand the school's competence base:* A business school needs to understand its competence base, what types of propositional knowledge it possesses, on both an individual basis and a combined basis. It is only through some understanding of this that it might realistically develop a strategy that builds on its strengths. Of course, this will also help with faculty recruitment, as the school will know what gaps need to be filled in order to be more successful in implementing its strategies, including that of strengthening a meaningful set of institutional learning partnerships. (We shall address the issue of faculty recruitment to achieve stronger institutional learning in Chapter 6.) A strategy that would ensure a realistic competence base for the school is likely to be fundamentally less discipline-focused and more learning partnership-oriented, eclectic and pioneering. This seems to be a requirement for today's value-creating learning organizations – leading corporations and top business schools alike.

4. *Choose a destiny:* The above discussion raises a further question. Can business schools choose a strategic direction or are they merely pulled or pushed by changes in the corporate environment over which they have little or no control? Schools need to move from fundamentally adapting to new realities to proactively shaping the agenda of the future. In doing so, they need to lead and be led. However, schools need to guard against choosing learning partners opportunistically, say because they are the "flavor of the month" at a particular time. True institutional learning must be based on a school's competencies, which allow it to develop cutting-edge propositional knowledge – seeing opportunities for further evolution of this knowledge base where others do not, and attempting to mobilize internal faculty resources to pursue these opportunities. It goes without saying that the faculty must find

this interesting – if they do not, there is no way to mobilize them! This type of institutional learning takes place through:

- Re-evaluating or changing strategy or the direction of learning within an established frame of propositional, research-based references.

- Re-evaluating or changing the frame of reference for problem definition and learning, allowing the established frame of propositional references to evolve as a consequence of learning through interaction with practice and the prescriptive knowledge that this generates.

- Learning to learn, finding out under what conditions organizations – both firms and business schools – are most likely to learn. This too might shape the business school's strategy, based on a plea for a focus on realistic areas.

5. *Focus on integration for academic value-creation:* Business schools are beginning to understand how learning patterns are changing for their learning partners. The key criterion of success for a business school – its mission – is to create value. For business school leaders to set strategic direction effectively, they must worry about creating value by emphasizing and integrating research, teaching and being actively involved with executives in their learning partner companies. As we have noted, executives and companies are a constant source of institutional learning. Collaborating with them outside the classroom helps define the research agenda, which results in faculty output that is more relevant to practicing managers. As discussed throughout this book, this means lead and be led, i.e. the interaction between propositional and prescriptive knowledge.

In sum, business schools must transform themselves from being fundamentally a collection of individuals to being more of a team-based provider of academic value-creation. The propositional knowledge bases that rest within the school must be shared among several professors in order to create a strong base of institutional knowledge.

Institutional learning at IMD

As noted, IMD has put most of its emphasis on executive development, complemented by a high-quality MBA offering, but without undergraduate or PhD programs. There thus seems to be a rather targeted academic value-creation focus at IMD, in contrast to most business schools, which typically have a much broader set of program activities. This added complexity typically might mean diversity in sub-cultures, a multidisciplinary focus, more sources of input from various types of students-cum-learners, etc. But it might also lead to a "centrifugal effect," creating dispersion or separate silos that do not work together! One might indeed expect that institutional learning would be more difficult in such settings. By contrast, the unifying perspective of IMD's executive development focus is likely to be a factor that might facilitate institutional learning within IMD.

But is this targeted niche enough to allow for the creation of true cutting-edge academic value? We think so, based, above all, on the realization that much of the change, innovation and progress today comes from leading firms. Also, we must realize that such firms, including leading consultants, are often in an excellent position to attract the best human talent – they certainly do not come to business schools as a given, or indeed to just any old business school! It is perhaps the variety of relationships with leading learning partners that will be key today, to ensure a strong lead and be led process – a rich interchange between propositional knowledge and prescriptive knowledge – and a sound base for institutional learning.

A factor that might add complexity to IMD's institutional learning is the very fact that it has to integrate rather complex multicountry and comparative cultural perspectives. But this is exactly what we are striving for! This type of complexity provides intellectual challenges that have the potential to *unify* the faculty. Many of the research areas can be applied across firms, cultures and countries. The propositional knowledge base does not have to be fragmented. And the leading executives from this globally diverse talent base will ensure that the prescriptive knowledge brought forward is truly challenging. So, the cross-cultural executive learning dimension *adds* focus, even though the context may seem diverse.

6 Human resources strategy

> Just as real business challenges are not neatly divided into academic disciplines, so our work at business schools, in both teaching and research, must blend the insights and expertise of many different fields. If schools are to remain relevant to the practice of business, they must be able to transcend the limitations of a strict discipline-focused approach.
>
> Jay Light, dean, Harvard Business School[1]

KEY POINTS

- The attraction, development and retention of the best possible faculty – and staff – are probably the most critical success factors for a business school.
- New team members must fit with the established culture – team players rather than individualists – and they should be at the cutting edge in their ability to engage in thought leadership. They should also add to the school's capabilities to engage in the types of institutional learning relationships that it has chosen to pursue.
- Business schools that avoid the typical structures of classic academic institutions – with their academic departments (silos), title hierarchies and tenure – are both a major attraction for many productive academics at other schools *and* a way to create positive institutional energy: little or no politics, no unnecessary committees, no seniority differentials and the like.
- A feedback and bonus system should be put in place that gives individual faculty members a chance to regularly – say twice a year – discuss their plans, performance, development issues and constraints with the school's leadership. There should also be a clear set of faculty incentives for the overall team and a bonus for meeting clear economic targets for the school. These bonuses may

---

[1] "Interview with Jay Light, Dean of Harvard Business School," *People's Daily Online* (May 15, 2007), english.people.com.cn/200705/15/eng20070515_374741.html (accessed June 6, 2007).

be awarded once per year. And they should be tailored to individual faculty members – to stimulate contributions in the areas where each of them is strong. Also, as the faculty member's interests and priorities change over time, the feedback and bonus system should also evolve.

- The hiring of new colleagues is clearly a faculty issue and priority – as well as a concern. While all must be involved, there is, nevertheless, a need for discretion – hence a special role for a faculty recruitment committee. When it comes to promotions and dismissals, the head of the school should play a driving role – committee work here would only lead to indecision and politics!
- Sabbaticals can be an important source of intellectual renewal for a faculty member, but they should only be given for a clear academic value-creation purpose – say to complete a book, article or other research project. Sabbaticals do not come "as an automatic and regular right," which in an extreme case might lead to a faculty member "sitting on the beach."

INTRODUCTION

The knowledge revolution is gaining momentum, with far-reaching strategic implications for organizations in both the corporate and private sectors. More than ever before, knowledge itself is an essential element of value-creation within an organization. And, since human capital is increasingly seen as the key asset in the value-creation equation, high quality human capital, with a relevant knowledge base, is vital. Thus, strategic human resources (HR) management will be essential for business schools to be more competitive, effective and, in the end, successful.

In this chapter, we will deal with the professorial HR base in business schools. It is understood that in any academic institution – business schools included – the professors must be of top quality. Without their drive for enhancing academic value-creation, generating cutting-edge research, leading the teaching and building strong relationships with students and executive participants, there will be little basis for success. Obviously, the other employees are important too. The administration must be outstanding, as must the research associates, the finance staff, the marketing team and so on. Still, in order to be able to contribute to the overall success of the academic institution, all of these other functions depend on an outstanding professorial staff.

FACULTY INVOLVEMENT

The faculty's involvement, when it comes to the HR strategy of a business school, is of course essential. In a way, the HR policy and strategy *is* the faculty's own set of issues. It is all about them! How, then, should the faculty be involved in setting strategic direction when it comes to HR policies as well as other related issues? How can such involvement be achieved without "abusing" faculty members' time and energy so that they can continue to carry out research and innovative teaching? How can such involvement be achieved without them becoming overly bogged down in endless committee work, corridor politics and the like, so that a strong dynamic drive is maintained within the school? Finally, should the faculty be involved in managing core administrative staff? Clearly, many of the tasks performed by the administrative staff have a direct impact on the faculty, but if professors assume responsibility for managing the staff, this could easily take too much time and energy away from their core tasks of conducting research and delivering innovative teaching, and thus seriously jeopardize the academic value-creation process.

> ### Faculty involvement in HR policies at IMD
> At IMD, faculty members play an important role in both the management committee and the faculty recruitment committee. These committees have a major impact on the development of the overall strategies of the school, including its HR strategies. The specific workings of these two committees are discussed later in the chapter.

In addition, important *ad hoc* faculty committees are formed at irregular intervals to stimulate broad-based discussions among the faculty on issues of key concern. One such committee recently dealt with IMD's business model for the future. What types of educational activities might IMD undertake in the future? What might the competition look like? What types of competencies would be needed at IMD? How much growth – top line as well as bottom line – would be desirable? This committee, consisting of six faculty members, consulted widely with a broad range of IMD's professors and subsequently led discussions on these topics at several faculty meetings. The result was a healthy view of how "good can be made even better" when it comes to the evolution of IMD's "business" mix.

A similar *ad hoc* committee dealt with the revision of IMD's faculty policies, as discussed later. Here, too, there was broad consultation and healthy plenary discussions at faculty meetings. Again, the faculty played a major role in reshaping the fundamentals of the school's policies.

It is clear that broad faculty involvement is not only desirable but also necessary. In the sense that one can meaningfully talk about the "ownership" of a business school, the faculty is the "owner." Hence, involvement is key. However, it should also be kept in mind that faculty time must not be "abused" by involving professors in too many tasks that might sap their time and energy. Administrative bureaucracy, therefore, should be avoided. There should be meaningful guidelines for the faculty to adhere to in a responsible way. As General Schwarzkopf put it, "When in doubt . . . do the right thing!"[2]

Hiring and firing decisions can become very political if they are done by committees. Consequently, it seems critical

---

[2] H. N. Schwarzkopf, *It doesn't take a hero: The autobiography* (New York: Bantam, 1992).

that strong leadership is in place. But how should this leadership function be monitored? What happens if, for example, the
new leader of a business school starts making bad termination
choices? Who defines what bad choices are? How is a termination dealt with? And how quickly does this happen in an
extreme case? I have few clear answers to these questions.
Clearly, the board must be involved, and there must be a regular
performance review. Clearly, also, a school's faculty-dominated
processes for hiring new members to join the team should give
some guarantee that poor hiring decisions can be avoided. But,
in the end, a school's success seems to be conspicuously depend-
ant on a progressive leader at the top.

LINKING THE HR STRATEGY TO THE OVERALL STRATEGY

Obviously, the HR strategy should be linked to the overall strategy
of the business school. However, in recent years, several strategic
changes seem to have been taking place in many business schools,
particularly with regard to research, teaching and citizenship. The
question is to what extent these shifts have affected professorial HR
strategies.

Research

As we discussed in Chapters 3 and 5, the classic approach to
research, where each discipline focuses on the specific in-depth
issues that are central to its own concerns, may no longer meet
the needs of learning partners. Cross-functional viewpoints are
becoming more critical, thus, the need for cross-functional, cross-
disciplinary research is greater than ever before. Of course, this will
have important implications for the hiring, promotion and retention
of professors. Different faculty capabilities are required, and faculty
must work effectively with other professors – a "we, we, we" attitude is required, rather than a "me, me, me" one. Or, as George
Buckley, chairman, president and CEO of 3M says, "We value

individual creativity, but we value team work equally. Giant egos are not welcomed."[3]

And today's professors must be able to "listen" to business practice and not come across as top-down, one-way disseminators of knowledge. They must be truly committed to exposing their proposition-based thought leadership to the best of practice, and they must take the prescriptive knowledge seriously! Not all academicians are able – or willing – to operate in this lead and be led way. Avoiding egotistical faculty candidates is, therefore, crucial.

It follows, as already discussed, that assessing research output might also differ from traditional practices, where there is often heavy emphasis on publishing articles in refereed axiomatic journals. Instead, new collected works in the form of research monographs, edited books that bring together a collection of research papers, and the like probably should be given more weight. Thus, the assessment of what constitutes good performance when it comes to a professor's research output is likely to be based on a broader set of research dimensions. This means that the process of assessing research output will become more complex. It is no longer enough to total up the number of refereed journal articles published by a professor in a given year.

IMD and multidisciplinary research

At IMD, joint authorship – reflecting the process of several professors working together on research projects – is well accepted. Single-author articles do not "count" more than joint works as such – it is the quality of the particular contribution that matters. This is perhaps close to what was attempted at the Carnegie Institute of Technology Business School in Pittsburgh in the early 1960s, where seminal scholars such as Herbert Simon, James March, Richard Cyert and Michael Cohen were active. At the time, this was considered fairly

---

[3] G. Buckley, Presentation at the Nikkei/Stanford/IMD Top Leadership Seminar, Tokyo (October 28, 2006).

avant-garde, although it is now much more common, certainly among many business schools that want to be at the forefront.

Teaching

Increasingly, we see a stronger link between research and teaching – as noted throughout this book – based on the symbiosis between propositional knowledge (from research) and prescriptive knowledge (from practice). The academic value-creation process is thus more closely linked with the practitioner's world. With the move toward a more cross-functional focus for research, it follows that there should be a similar emphasis when it comes to teaching. Executive program participants can provide significant prescriptive insights when it comes to both research and teaching. This process of leading as well as being led, of speaking as well as listening, is likely to result in teaching that is more easily understood in practical terms and, consequently, more immediately relevant to learning partners.

Thus, the criteria for judging a professor's teaching performance, like those for assessing research performance, will likely change dramatically. There will be more of a focus on cross-functional, practically oriented teaching capabilities and the ability to communicate more effectively with learning partners – listening and give-and-take will be key.

Practice-oriented teaching: IMD's Booster program

The Booster program is both a program and something more like a consulting project. It is also a hybrid of an open and a customized program. It has been designed for company teams – typically cross-functional management teams – that have to tackle a concrete business challenge. One example of such a challenge might be "how to effectively introduce the company's latest innovation into a global marketplace." In the Booster program, learning and preparing for the implementation of these new insights in a participant's own company are blended together.

Before the five-day program on campus, IMD helps each team of participants with project definition, data collection, structuring issues and team building. This phase typically includes one or two days with program faculty and four or five days' support from an IMD project manager. The goal of this phase is to help the team "hit the ground running" during the week at IMD.

During the program, the company teams receive faculty input on general topics, such as improving leadership, teamwork, networking skills, innovation and execution. The participants follow plenary sessions with all company teams present, so that they also can learn from the best prescriptive practices of other firms. They then break into small groups to continue work with peers from other companies. When they come back into their company teams, they apply their new insights to their project.

At the end of the program, the teams present an action plan to their respective company sponsors (usually the CEO or another member of the senior management team).

The optional post-program phase concentrates on team effectiveness, project progress monitoring and addressing the execution barriers that teams typically face after they return to the office. Again, program faculty and project managers work in partnership to support the ongoing success of the project.

Citizenship

By "citizenship," I mean the link between professors and program participants and, increasingly, with their companies. Again, it seems as if two-way interaction is called for, with the professor playing an active role in terms of listening, learning and addressing what learning partners – as the representatives of their companies – need to know. In a wider context, citizenship also means that professors should take ownership of the wellbeing of the school as a whole, not just their own wellbeing or that of their discipline. New criteria may be needed for judging a professor's performance when it comes to citizenship – with a particular focus on a demonstrated interest in the participants, corporations, the broader needs of the business school and the ability/willingness to listen, as well as to give feedback.

A way to think about the citizenship responsibilities is to consider it as part of service management – after all a business school can be considered to be in the service sector! It should be stressed that faculty members will be expected to balance their time among all three – research, teaching *and* citizenship. To ignore the citizenship side is not an option! When it comes to being at odds with the school's predominant values and culture, i.e. citizenship, there must be a real cost when it comes to the bonus for those who are not team players in this respect.

Faculty citizenship at IMD

Good citizenship, engaging with participants and other faculty in and around the classroom, is not enough at IMD. We expect faculty to be active in communicating IMD's fortes to the world. IMD professors may be called upon to accompany field representatives on company visits or to business forums or alumni meetings. They may also get involved in new faculty recruitment. And their presence at faculty meetings and faculty retreats is expected of all – citizenship implies that all, in the end, are responsible for the school. All members of the faculty are thus expected also to play a role in making IMD work as a business.

Fundamentally speaking, citizenship means committing to developing a one-team culture. This means that citizenship would emphasize that faculty members must be inclusive rather than exclusive in forming teams. They would also be expected to help find opportunities to integrate new faculty members effectively into the overall team. Good citizenship thus means avoiding a "win-lose" type of competition between faculty members. It is not a matter of excelling at the expense of others.

This team commitment certainly also involves having a physical presence at IMD, but it goes beyond this. It has more to do with a substantive commitment toward meaningful, value-creating activities at IMD, such as accessibility, flexibility and positive collegial involvement. As already mentioned, it is the team's responsibility to contribute to business development and strong learning partner relations.

Hiring and promotion

It goes without saying that it is critical for business schools to hire the best professorial talent that can be found and to promote only those talents that truly contribute to the success of the school. Typically, this will be achieved through careful pre-screening and committees of faculty members making initial assessments. This will then be followed by a campus visit from the prospective candidate, including one-on-one interviews and research/practitioner-oriented presentations. Based on this, the school will make its choice, usually after a rather elaborate, often difficult, set of discussions within a designated faculty committee in charge of the narrowing down process.

The difference nowadays will be in terms of the criteria used to evaluate good research (more cross-functional, more team-oriented, less axiomatic, less individualistic), teaching (more practitioner-oriented, more interactive, less axiomatic, less narrow) and citizenship. It will typically be much more difficult, therefore, to make the optimal professorial choices – there are more criteria to consider and more often these point in opposite directions. It is a matter of handling these situations as dilemmas, rather than trying to find someone who scores "best" on everything! There is, also, often a need to involve not only more faculty but also staff in the process.

When it comes to promotion, similar issues come into play, i.e. focusing on promoting faculty members who can truly contribute in terms of research, teaching and citizenship within the parameters of the new strategic direction. Promotions, particularly those that result in tenure, can typically be rather "political." Different faculty members may have different views of what constitutes good research, teaching and citizenship, and these views are often shaped by the past. To a greater or lesser extent, a given faculty member may, for instance, have been brought up in a more axiomatically driven world, and it may indeed be difficult for him or her to adjust fully to the new strategic direction of the business school. Consequently, the faculty member might – deliberately or inadvertently – apply criteria that would have been more suitable in the past.

As it is more important than ever for business schools to be able to attract the best talent available, they will need to pay competitive salaries. At many business schools, faculty compensation is fixed and/or tied to seniority. Often, this fixed pay is rather poor, consistent with the norms of public sector administration, which perhaps reflects the fact that many business schools tend to rely on public funding. As an incentive for faculty to focus on outstanding research, teaching and citizenship, as described earlier, it would seem logical to have a compensation plan that includes a bonus based on performance in these areas. The bonus should be earned every year, with no automatic pay increase due to seniority – good performance must be repeated on an annual basis to qualify for the bonus.

All in all, the pay for an active, well-performing professor should be good. Ways to achieve this would vary for each individual – some focusing relatively more on research, others relatively more on teaching. Flexibility is a key dimension of compensation. Although the pay could be quite generous when individual performance is good, it is nevertheless unlikely that an academic institution will be able to compete fully with related fields, such as consulting. Therefore, a basic commitment to an academic career must always be there!

INITIAL CAREER CHOICE FOR A FACULTY MEMBER STARTING OUT

I have prescribed a process of academic value-creation based on thought leadership – propositional knowledge from research, which would meet the prescriptive knowledge from the best of practice. For academia to play its role here, there would be a call for more eclecticism, rather than so much focus on the traditional axiomatic disciplines. For young academics starting their careers, this can represent a challenge – even a difficult hurdle. Often, they will not have received appropriate training to achieve this. It is typically easier – and more predictable in terms of finishing – to receive a doctoral degree within the axiomatic/disciplinary model frame. And indeed this is what is typically offered. The same is true when it comes to choosing a first academic position – it is probably easier to follow the classical axiomatic route, with relatively well-defined promotional paths, often with tenure based on publishing in the "right" journals as the culmination.

Thus, it might be hard, or almost impossible, for the younger academic to justify becoming part of the prescribed process for eclectic academic value-creation advocated in this book. Maybe it would be "safer" to "first get tenure somewhere else and then come to a place such as IMD!" This would also give the young academic a strong base for developing his or her practical, managerial experience further, also a virtual requirement for playing an effective value-creating role in the new context.

FRAGMENTATION OF ACADEMIC VALUE-CREATING TASKS

If one follows the arguments of this book, then teaching and research go together. This means that *one* faculty should undertake *both* research *and* teaching. One side is essential for the other, and vice versa, for effective academic value-creation. It follows, therefore, that meaningful teaching – including teaching executives – should also be part of a faculty member's workload.

Surprisingly, there are situations where the above does not apply. For instance, in some academic institutions, executive education teaching is done as an "extra activity for extra remuneration," and only by some faculty members. The "real" teaching is delivered to the MBAs, doctoral students and undergraduates. As we have argued, the executive education arena perhaps offers the most unique opportunity for academic value-creation by bringing research and leading executives together from all over the world, thereby providing a true exchange of propositional and prescriptive knowledge. It is ironic, however, that this type of teaching is sometimes not treated with the same institutional commitment as other teaching activities. Implying that it is less valuable within an academic community/team undercuts the very essence of modern academic value-creation, where executive education teaching probably should be at the center – at least in the modern business school!

Perhaps even worse, there are also academic institutions where the "main" faculty consists of professors, often organized along rather axiomatic departmental lines, with a full hierarchy of titles and a corresponding tenure-based promotional process. They are complemented by an *ad hoc* teaching faculty, often consisting of practice professors, part-time professors, leading executives and the like, who typically undertake most of the teaching. Thus, a *split* between research and teaching has been created. Hence, also, the key driver for academic value-creation, namely the effective *interplay* between propositional and prescriptive knowledge, would be gone.

Proponents of this split system might argue that it could make it easier to attract and retain professors if they are given a context of classical "values" so that they know that the individual "publish or perish" is what counts. It seems to me that this would not be a strong argument if it were to result in the research becoming less relevant.

Equally questionable would be the fact that much of the teaching would be undertaken in this type of a system *without* the necessary research base to truly stimulate outstanding groups of executives from all over the world – a sub-optimal situation.

There might even be further fragmentation of tasks in some academic institutions. For instance, case writers might lead a "life of their own," developing teaching materials that are not necessarily linked to research or not sufficiently integrated into the pedagogical task in the classroom. When research associates and case writers are used, it is critical that they are closely linked into the rest of the academic value-creation process, i.e. into both the research and the pedagogical/teaching side. Often this is not the case.

The result of all of this is the fragmentation of academic value-creating tasks and, in the end, a less effective academic value-creation process.

IMPLICATIONS FOR BUSINESS SCHOOLS

In this chapter, I have argued for a performance-based HR strategy that is linked to the overall strategy of the business school. An HR strategy along these lines would probably benefit from the dissolution of academic departments, the abolition of academic titles and the related hierarchy, and even the abandonment of tenure! I have advocated a performance-based bonus system for each faculty member, and I have suggested guidelines for structuring such an approach. But, in the end, the success of the business school will, of course, depend more on creating a climate where committed faculty members are encouraged to learn and develop their full potential than it will on formal HR guidelines.

1. *An actively involved dean is required:* The professorial HR strategy in a business school is increasingly becoming a key element of success. And linking the HR strategy to the overall strategy of the school requires a strong commitment on the part of the dean and other academic leaders in the school. Furthermore, the implementation of the strategy requires an element of managerial judgment, and this means that the dean, perhaps together with one or more associate deans, should be actively involved in the process. This is particularly true when it comes to performance reviews, promotions, setting bonuses and the like. Also, it would be preferable for one person to have full responsibility for specific

aspects of the performance assessments to avoid "committee decisions" that typically end in compromises, often more convenience-driven than strategy-driven.

2. *Academic values must guide the HR strategy:* It is important to make sure that it is the fundamental values of the academic institution that drive the HR strategy and not mere formality or strict legality. These values need to be the key guiding light for the dean, as well as for other academic members. Having too many bureaucratic rules will simply not work. Long lists of written guidelines, constant committee meetings and politically motivated decisions can only lead to divisiveness and, ultimately, lack of academic progress. Each individual faculty member must be given the freedom to excel, and this is what the HR strategy must promote.

3. *HR procedures and guidelines are still critical:* They should be spelled out in detail when it comes to:
   - Hiring and contract renewal decisions
   - Procedure for asking a faculty member to leave
   - Faculty consulting, to avoid faculty members competing with their own institution
   - Bonus assessment for research, teaching and citizenship performance
   - Guidelines for extra pay for extra work

   A concern for equity must drive all of this. All faculty members must feel that they are being treated equitably – this leads to trust, which is critical. Some faculty members, of course, may want to test the limits of procedures and guidelines. It is important that they can relate corrective actions from the school's leadership back to the procedures and guidelines – so that they can sense that they are not being singled out "for special treatment."

4. *Freedom to recruit professors from anywhere:* It is essential to be able to recruit the best professors, no matter where they come from. This requires open recruitment procedures and a counterbalancing of the tendency to consider only candidates from one's

local community as eligible for positions. Typically, this means
that leading professors will, to a greater extent, be invited to join
an academic organization and that there will be fewer open application processes. The current practice, where many countries
"reserve" professorships for their own citizens, would have to
change.

5. *Minimalist organizational structure:* Business schools have typically developed internal organizational structures around functional disciplines. These structural solutions have perhaps largely
served the interests of the faculty. Unfortunately, this internal
view is perhaps less than optimal when it comes to finding
organizational structures that can serve modern learning partners
and help the school to function in the modern environment. I
recommend the following modifications:

- *Fewer or no academic departments:* It is vital that professors
organize themselves on an *ad hoc* basis in response to the
needs of the clients – for teaching program initiatives as well
as for research. This means that the teaching and/or research
teams will typically be multidisciplinary and cross functional. A key element of the HR strategy should be to place
a premium on open cooperation among faculty members –
silos should be discouraged. The classic departmental structure, with its focus on pursuing disciplinary specialization,
may work against this. In order to encourage more eclectic
research and teaching, business schools might consider combining academic departments so that they span broader academic disciplines. Then again, perhaps the more logical
solution would be to abandon all academic departments. Of
course, the practicality of this would depend on the size of
the business school. In a large institution, there may be some
need for a departmental structure. Interestingly, therefore, a
future trend might perhaps be toward smaller business
schools, each with an *ad hoc* organizational structure based
on eclectic activities.

- *Simplified title hierarchy:* Placing a premium on brains on an ongoing basis is fundamental to the modern business school. Academic excellence assumes that people with relevant competencies complement each other in teams. In this type of "flat" organization, the classic title hierarchy would mean less and less. Seniority would simply not apply. Unfortunately, however, there is typically a rather well-established seniority system in most academic institutions, which is often reinforced by a hierarchy of academic titles. This tends to result in senior professors having somewhat more privileged positions relative to their younger colleagues. Seniority *per se,* however, does not necessarily equate with ongoing performance. The logical extension of this, when it comes to an HR strategy in an academic institution, is probably to get rid of academic titles. Ideally, all members of the academic team should have the same title so that it is clear that it is ongoing performance on a day-to-day basis, and not simply seniority that dictates how well a professor is doing. Again, this would probably also call for somewhat smaller academic institutions or for relatively self-contained academic entities. It would be important to understand "who is who" within the academic team, but one would not need titles to "peg" people to performance.

    No tenure: Stimulating sustainable performance for each professor over time is critical for ongoing academic excellence, and this should be a key part of the HR strategy for any business school. However, tenure, which was perhaps a legitimate phenomenon in the past, might contribute to an attitude of complacency and inactivity. Abandoning tenure would seem to be a reasonable way to avoid this. If a professor is no longer able to provide relevant inputs, one might argue that he or she should be asked to leave. Also, without tenure, the professors themselves will feel more pressure to stay relevant, to contribute and to provide value. A business school with no tenure, of course, would need to have clear policies on how to judge performance criteria and procedures for termination.

6. *Competitive compensation:* The fixed salary of each professor should be competitive relative to other business schools – no more, no less. In addition, the difference in fixed salary levels between senior members of the faculty team and more junior members should be relatively small, i.e. a rather compressed fixed salary scale. This would signal that all professors – regardless of seniority – belong to one team.

7. *Performance-based bonus:* An annual group bonus, based on the overall performance of the academic institution, would signify the need for all the faculty members to work together. It would also make it crystal clear to the individual faculty members that they are part of a team. Equally important is an individual bonus based on tangible research output – not research plans or work in progress. Lack of realism and wishful thinking on the part of individual faculty members can easily drive the latter! A concrete set of research output would typically qualify for a bonus.

The individual bonus would also take into account teaching performance, with a focus on teaching innovation (as opposed to "good" teaching, which is a given) and with a minimal time lag in bringing new research findings into the classroom. When it comes to innovation, the short-term ratings by the participants of each class session can have a counterproductive effect. Some faculty members may prefer to provide "safe," previously tested materials, rather than providing new ones that reflect their thought leadership and the research momentum. New materials, by their very nature, always carry a certain risk that they are not polished enough to rate well with the participants.

As mentioned in Chapter 2, IMD has pioneered a way to try to counterbalance this type of conservatism with its annual Orchestrating Winning Performance (OWP) program. It involves the entire faculty who are expected to present entirely new materials to the 500+ participants. The institutional expectation that every faculty member develop new materials for this program also tends to speed up innovation and the drive toward the constant renewal of IMD's open programs in general.

In addition to research and teaching, the individual bonus would also be awarded for citizenship, i.e. being accessible to and working with learning partners, meeting potential clients and being proactive when it comes to "marketing" the school.

8. *Clear guidelines for faculty consulting:* Human resources guidelines should be developed so that individual professors cannot compete with their own business school, say by offering programs privately that legitimately should be part of the school's offerings. After all, the institution provides the research funding for the individual professors to remain at the cutting edge. Thus, it would not be acceptable for a professor to take this cutting-edge knowledge and offer it on a private basis.

It is important that any faculty consulting guidelines allow the boundaries between the business school's activities and what is considered private faculty consulting to evolve. Such an evolutionary approach is consistent with the need to be flexible when it comes to serving leading learning partner firms. One useful guideline here would be for faculty to ask for permission for all consulting activities that are concerned with existing or immediate past learning partners of the business school. Faculty will benefit from consulting policies that are clear, unambiguous and operational, so that the transaction costs of enforcing them can be minimized. Beyond this, when it comes to cases that might be less cut and dried, a good principle would be to clear any consulting work with the school's leadership upfront. Over time, broadly shared healthy norms can thereby evolve.

At IMD, we feel that if we are to have a sustainable business model the school cannot allow faculty to compete directly with the school for private consulting opportunities. A more *laissez-faire* consulting policy existed a few decades ago, and it led to a lot of conflict.

Everyone at IMD also understands that the consulting policies must be enforced by the president/dean. This means that they must be clear enough to be enforceable, and the school's leadership must demonstrate the *will* to enforce them. Each faculty member reports his or her consulting activities every six months, as part of the biannual faculty review with the president/dean and senior associate dean. This report also indicates the plans for the next six months. A maximum of forty-five days per year of consulting is allowed.

9. *Faculty workload:* There are standard norms for what constitutes an expected workload for faculty. At IMD, this is set at ninety days. This does not in fact mean "days" in the normal sense of the word. Rather, it means a half day in the classroom for which it is assumed that a half day of preparation is required to equal a full day. For the school to be able to deliver on all of its programs, each faculty member is expected to pick up a mix of longer and shorter teaching assignments. By sharing the workload in this way, an overall balance is achieved. When faculty members have several sessions within a given program, they will more likely be able to enter into an effective process of two-way learning with the participants. There are, however, often situations where a faculty member will be called on to give only one or two sessions in a program. In these cases, it will be less likely, under normal circumstances, to achieve the desired lead and be led effect fully.

What drives the mix of assignments has to do with the need to come up with meaningful course offerings, consisting of a cross-section of topics to be covered by various faculty members with a pedagogical flow that achieves high dynamism in the program (typically not so easily done if one faculty member monopolizes the program). The challenge with all of this is that a typical faculty workload can lead to a rather "chopped up" work situation. This fragmentation can pose a challenge to the research execution expected of each faculty member. It is, therefore, particularly important that a faculty member possess the ability and discipline to use all free time to be productive, even when these windows are relatively small.

It will typically be desirable that the workload for any faculty member be characterized by diversity – variety to satisfy a faculty member's need for meaningful development challenges. Monotony and repetitiveness would be dysfunctional. Good faculty members like variety!

It is understood that the intensity of the research and teaching load at a business school such as IMD can be exhausting for faculty members. Thus, as discussed, it is important that sabbaticals be offered to faculty, as required, to complete particular research projects and to counterbalance any sense of fatigue or even burnout. However, it should be reinforced that sabbaticals should not constitute an automatic calendar-driven "right" for faculty members; they must justify them based on completing a research project.

Business schools might also benefit from "buying back" individual faculty time for additional teaching, i.e. days initially allowed for individual consulting, so that the "investment" made in that professor's research knowledge can be further leveraged by the school. There should be an upper limit, however, to extra teaching to avoid the risk of the professor "burning out." Clearly, this is typically a win-win proposition, of equal benefit to the professors and the school – as long as it is kept within reasonable limits.

10. *Transparency is key:* To ensure successful implementation of the HR strategy, total transparency is vital. But it must be done in a way that does not compromise an individual's right to personal data protection. This might mean that bonuses, salary levels and the like would be indicated broadly in ranges or bands, so that individual professors could easily check where they fit into the various bands, without revealing their personal information. It would also mean that teaching loads should be broadly published so that no "me, me, me" freeloaders go undetected. With luck,

the "new" transparent culture might mean that freeloaders will be subjected to group pressure from their colleagues. Transparency regarding teaching would clearly also be needed to allow for clarity when it comes to additional individual pay for doing more teaching than normal, so that all professors can feel that they are participating in a fair way in terms of this additional source of income.

And there should be transparency concerning "who receives what" when it comes to R&D support. In total, there should be a strong sense of openness when it comes to distribution of "duties" as well as benefits, so that there is an overall sense of fairness among all members of the faculty team.

Transparency and equity are of course highly related issues. Transparency helps in communicating equity – and helps to ensure it!

IMD's human resources strategy

IMD's HR strategy, with regard to recruitment, organizational structure, compensation and support, is really quite simple – it reflects IMD's rather focused strategy and the strong belief in minimalist approaches to structural issues:

Recruitment: IMD's president chairs the faculty recruitment committee, which consists of seven faculty members. Rather than looking for professors to fill slots, IMD selects faculty who will add academic value, given IMD's broader needs, and who fit IMD's business model of pursuing learning partnerships, practitioner-relevant research and pedagogical delivery. Candidates must show an ability to lead and to be led.

After interviews and campus visits, candidates are asked to present their expertise to an audience of IMD faculty and research staff, who subsequently give their feedback to the faculty recruitment committee. One potential dysfunctional effect that should be guarded against during the recruitment process is "blackballing," i.e. some internal faculty members finding that there is something "wrong" with almost all candidates who present themselves. "No one is good enough for IMD!" Ironically, many faculty members taking such a stand would not have been hired themselves if such inflexible criteria had been applied to them. It is, therefore, important that everyone keep an open mind so that exceptional talent can be identified. This does not always follow the conventional lines of what might be an acceptable new faculty recruit. For this reason, it is also important that, in the end, IMD's president/dean have the final word, even though he rarely, if ever, would go against the views of the majority of the faculty and the recruitment committee. The same principle applies to how visiting faculty are treated while at IMD, which should always be with respect. Only then will IMD's options be open to the maximum!

The right candidates will get a three-year contract. In these three years, they get the chance to prove their worth to the institution, the Learning Network and the participants. If all is well, the first three-year contract is renewed for another three years, and subsequently becomes open-ended. This means that the faculty member's employment can be terminated with one year's notice – but of course only in exceptional circumstances.

Organizational structure: There are no academic departments – every IMD professor has to be ready to collaborate with every other professor, be it in research or in teaching. All faculty carry the title of professor; there are no hierarchical titles that distinguish one professor from another. Tenure does not exist at IMD, as can be deduced from the previous section. Year on year, professors, no matter how senior, have to prove their value as active members of the IMD community – to colleagues and to learning partners and their companies.

Performance assessment and bonuses: A nine-member executive committee of IMD's foundation board determines the absolute amount of bonus money available to the faculty for the year. This amount depends on IMD's financial health. In 2006, the committee allocated 36 per cent of fixed salary costs for bonuses. Members of IMD's faculty received a group bonus of 18 per cent (50 per cent of the 36 per cent) and an additional individual bonus that depended on their individual performance. Research output accounts for 50 per cent of the individual bonus. As IMD's president, once a year I review all publications, considering the value and quality of each. The other 50 per cent of the bonus is based on teaching innovation (30 per cent) and citizenship (20 per cent). IMD's associate dean makes these assessments. To gauge teaching innovation, he tracks new case usage by the author and by other professors, the class feedback ratings – every faculty session is evaluated by learning partner participants – and the citizenship activities of each faculty member. Here he counts relationship-building sessions with prospective and existing learning partners, delivery of presentations at alumni events and presence at faculty meetings and retreats, etc.

Supporting faculty: Every six months, IMD's associate dean and I meet individually with every member of the faculty team to follow their progress and provide support for their activities, just as a CEO would do with the members of his or her management team. We discuss research progress and specific progress with regard to teaching workload and class performance issues, development output, resource needs and anything else that will help the faculty advance in their academic value-creation and develop their full potential.

IMD's faculty guidelines: IMD has twelve faculty guidelines that describe the institute's practices with regard to workload, consulting, hiring and termination, procedures for the appointment of IMD's president, grievances, compensation, pension and the like. These guidelines are reviewed whenever deemed necessary and have recently been revised by a faculty team, then passed by an advisory vote of the faculty and finally a ratifying vote of the executive committee of the IMD foundation board.

7 The learning partner perspective

A moment's insight is sometimes worth a lifetime's experience.
Oliver Wendell Holmes, Jr., Associate Justice, US Supreme Court, 1902–32[1]

KEY POINTS
- It is vital for the CEO, senior management and a broad set of executives to act as catalysts to stimulate a learning culture and disseminate this culture broadly within the firm. Since most CEOs will be pushing their strategic change agendas, they will typically need to draw on executive learning to bring the executive cadres along so that they can effectively implement the new strategic directions. Thus, the creation of a learning culture would be a key item on the CEO's agenda.
- The HR function typically plays an important role in supporting the CEO and senior management. Apart from the obvious responsibility of hiring and developing new talent – perhaps through executive education programs – HR may also be responsible for implementing the mandate from top management for a strengthened corporate culture.
- The new role of chief learning officer (CLO) is increasingly being created as a specific, separate function to underscore the importance of lifelong learning and to ensure that learning tasks are not underemphasized because of HR's other pressing activities. In particular, the CLO may be involved in developing tailored programs that will support the implementation of new strategic shifts mandated by senior management. Often the CLO is responsible for the "corporate university" in a firm.

---

[1] *The Quotations Page*, www.quotationspage.com/quotes/Oliver_Wendell_Holmes_Jr., accessed February 9, 2007.

- The menu of learning activities available to firms includes (1) open-enrollment executive programs, typically to support individuals in developing particular skills; (2) tailored, in-company executive programs, which tend to focus on implementing strategic changes as well as developing a more unified corporate culture; and (3) programs offered by corporate universities, where company-specific, and often sensitive strategic issues can be dealt with.

- Corporate universities, at their best, can be accelerators for a wide variety of learning. At their worst, however, they can lead to "inbreeding" and a less open view on learning. They may end up safeguarding the positions of particular executives who are assigned to the corporate university, and/or just aiming to "fill seats." Degeneration and stagnation may be the result.

- It is important to find a balance between quality and cost effectiveness. For instance, some companies might find it tempting to "cherry pick" individual professors to deliver *ad hoc* sessions in their corporate university, in order to keep costs down. But the quality of the learning might suffer, as it is not delivered as part of a cohesive package. Further, one might find that if the corporate procurement function is responsible for executive education, this can put relatively too much emphasis on the cost management side, at the expense of the learning quality side.

- For a company, developing a learning partnership with a leading business school can be a key component of a commitment to lifelong learning, but only if a true partnership is developed. Delegation of key learning activities – that is, senior management walking away from these tasks – cannot work.

- Action-oriented research – particularly on company-specific issues of internally generated growth and on more focused management processes – must also be driven by the firm itself. The business school can play a partnership role here – but the firm must be the key driver and agenda-setter.

INTRODUCTION

In all of the previous chapters, I have focused on the business school and its role and contributions when it comes to forming and sustaining partnerships between leading executives from best-practice corporations and academics in good business schools. Throughout these chapters, I have largely taken the viewpoint of professors in business schools and have discussed how *they* develop learning partnerships with business. In this chapter, I shall discuss the same set of topics, but from the point of view of the firm(s) and the practicing executives-cum-learning partners. What is different, from a company's perspective, when it comes to forming a learning partnership? While there are differences in emphasis, many of the issues, as we shall see, have already been well covered – hence the relatively short length of this chapter.

It seems particularly important that companies realize that learning may significantly contribute to value-creation. As the quote by Holmes at the beginning of this chapter suggests, executives are looking to business schools to deliver insights that might otherwise take them a lifetime of work experience to gain. A cornerstone of Holmes's judicial philosophy was his opinion that, "The life of the law has not been logic, but experience."[2] He convinced people that the law should develop along with the society it serves, and that the court should look at the facts in a changing society, instead of clinging to tired slogans and formulas. Business, too, needs to develop along with the society it serves. Therefore, companies must attempt to create and implement a learning culture on an ongoing basis, and responsibility for this must rest largely with top management. It cannot be wholly delegated to business schools, nor can it be subcontracted, say, to consulting firms that might specialize in learning. Delegating this task internally will typically not work either. For instance, it would be erroneous to think that by creating a corporate university, the special group of executives assigned to it would then take care of the lifelong learning task. It is the CEO, with his or her

---

[2] O. W. Holmes, Jr., *Common law* (Boston, MA: Little, Brown, and Company, 1881), 1.

executive team, who must drive corporate learning. And corporate learning is a mindset that must be shared among all layers of management, not just a few.

PARTNERSHIPS: WHAT CAN – AND SHOULD – LEADING FIRMS DO?

The paramount starting point is that the firm's top management should instill a culture of active lifelong learning in its executives. This implies that executives would largely be responsible for their own learning and that the firm would proactively encourage this, perhaps by coming up with a specific strategy to support them in their learning. While many firms rely on the individual initiatives and commitments of specific executives – perhaps backed up by the HR function, which might see specific development needs for particular executives – more and more corporations are now developing explicit learning strategies. Typically, these learning strategies will attempt to codify what type of learning can/should take place on the job – in addition, of course, to whatever further training needs there might be. Thus, learning also becomes part of the job charter of the individual executive. It is perhaps equally important that the person who manages the executive have, as part of her or his job description, responsibility for the executive's learning. Executive development becomes a task for all!

In addition to codifying the learning needs of individual executives and developing a corporate learning strategy, there are also often additional learning initiatives embedded in corporate universities. Typically, the activities of a corporate university tend to be heavily focused on developing a common culture within a given company. But practice varies widely from one corporation to another. Some will have elaborate set-ups under the label "corporate university" – others will not. Some corporations rely on their HR function to carry out these institutional learning initiatives. Others might have their own CLO, potentially with a dedicated staff, as a catalyst to spearhead learning. Let us now discuss these issues in more detail.

LEARNING ON THE JOB

Learning on the job will always be key, particularly in encouraging the sense of networking that stimulates the exchange of best practices *across* functions and plant and/or office sites, often in different countries. Eclecticism is at the heart of this. Creating a learning organization thus involves breaking down silos and encouraging broader, eclectic interaction. Of course, this has become much easier with the advent of the web.

IMD's Wednesday Webcasts, for example, offer an excellent vehicle to stimulate learning on the job for executives. In part, they can do this by simply viewing any webcast sessions they find interesting and reflecting on them on their own. They can also view the webcasts together with other executives, even from other parts of the firm, and then discuss what the implications might be. Dialogue might even take place virtually, via the web. And there are no limits to eclecticism here – executives from separate companies can even interact. This is, in many ways, analogous to the so-called quality circles, or *kaizen*, so prominent in Japan, for example. Exchange via the web could thus dramatically increase the potential for learning.

INDIVIDUAL DEVELOPMENT NEEDS

It is typically the responsibility of direct line managers to help identify when individual executives have unique development needs, often as part of an annual or semi-annual performance review meeting. The company's HR function would usually also be responsible for working with individual executives to find ways of meeting their unique learning needs. This might lead, for instance, to sending an individual to an open-enrollment program at a business school, or arranging for personal coaching.

Individual executive learning could also be focused on further developing specific values or norms. For instance, the corporate culture is becoming more and more important in many companies. Thus an in-house training program for groups of individuals can often be an effective way of instilling corporate values, such as teamwork ("we, we, we," not "me, me, me"); recognizing and dealing with matters in a forthright way rather than being overly "political"; focusing on an open interpersonal style; and relying less on organizational hierarchy and more on *ad hoc* teams in a "flat" organization. These types of cultural learning initiatives can also often be carried out under the auspices of a company's corporate university.

IMPLEMENTING STRATEGIC CHANGE

For many companies, the issue of rapidly implementing strategic change is becoming increasingly critical. Often, responsibility for this rests firmly with the CEO and, more than ever, it is the hallmark of his or her success. Therefore, the question of how to execute rapid strategic change has become critical. Of course, the CEO can always hand-pick executives who are seen as "doers" and place them in key implementational roles to speed up organizational change. Another way to do this is through organized executive development programs. Typically, the CEO might "commission" an in-company program to cover the critical change issues, and often be heavily involved in the design of the program as well as specify who will actually attend. For the CEO (as well as for the company), an additional benefit of commissioning a tailored executive program is that a relatively large number of executives can participate in the program within a reasonably short time, thus speeding up the pace of strategic implementation and change.

To add to the program's effectiveness, the CEO will typically also participate in its delivery, by, for instance, giving an overview of the current strategy and the key strategic change issues at hand. In some cases, the CEO might be a full participant in one of the programs. If the CEO is part of the program delivery team, ample time for questions and answers should be built in – a sign of open-mindedness! By participating in this way, the CEO can dramatically increase the commitment to implementation throughout the company. Commenting on a recent in-company program with Borealis, program director Martha Maznevski noted, "The executive board actually came as participants, which is not a usual practice. It sent a very strong signal that the top management believed learning is important. IMD likes to work with a partner that challenges and pushes, and Borealis certainly pushed to create challenges at IMD. Borealis has been a fantastic learning partner."[3]

Holcim is another example of a company that involves its senior management team. In the eight-day tailored program that IMD delivers for Holcim, each half day has a Holcim executive (including all of the executive committee) who helps transfer the learning back to Holcim through a presentation and question-and-answer session. Markus Akermann, the CEO, is usually there for both the opening and closing half days. The program is an excellent example of the interplay of propositional and prescriptive knowledge.

Often in such programs, teams work on specific strategic program assignments. At best, these assignments are consistent with what needs to be done to implement the new strategy. This action-learning component thus feeds directly into accelerating the strategic change agenda. Therefore, it might also be worthwhile for the CEO to listen to the team presentations when they elaborate on their "solutions." During the presentations, however, the CEO must be careful not to dominate the discussions or "steal ownership" of the ideas. Instead, he or she should actively participate by positioning him- or herself as a useful resource, thereby adding further to the quality of the action learning process. Above all, the CEO must show that he or she is genuine and sincere!

THE CORPORATE UNIVERSITY – DEVELOPING A CORPORATE CULTURE

Many companies have established their own in-house learning institutions that are responsible for a number of executive learning

---

[3] *Borealis Annual Report 2005*, www.borealisgroup.com/public/news/financial/ report_2005/print149.html (2005), accessed August 27, 2007.

issues. Increasingly, these have come to be known as "corporate universities." Whether or not to attach the "corporate university" label on them is perhaps a question of semantics. Clearly, they are not universities in the classic sense. The use of the name, however, symbolically indicates the high ambition and aspirations for the quality of learning that the corporation expects from this undertaking. Perhaps another important signal will be the fact that there might be a multitude of disciplinary approaches within a corporate university. Executives from various businesses and from various parts of the world might be involved. This underscores an eclectic commitment to learning, quite analogous to what can be found in a university.

There are many challenges when it comes to making a corporate university work well. For example, executives who have corporate learning as their full-time job will eventually be faced with their own "professional renewal." If this evolutionary renewal goes awry, corporate university executives might, over time, become conservative, burnt out and even contribute to the status quo – or worse – when it comes to delivering learning in the corporate university. At the very best, such as at General Electric's corporate university, the CEO and his or her team are heavily involved in the university and personally make sure that it is focused on the corporation's strategic priorities.

When the corporate university has invested in its own bricks and mortar, the potential threat of conservatism can become even more acute. Moreover, there may be more pressure to "fill seats," rather than to deliver the cutting-edge executive learning initiatives actually needed. The learning effectiveness may be further diminished by the pressure to use one's own facilities, even though a better option might be available elsewhere. The advantages of having one's own physical corporate facilities have thus become more doubtful recently, in that they may not be up to par with cutting-edge facilities at, say, leading business schools, which tend to have high ceilings, lots of natural light, work group space and the like.

As already noted, a corporate university can play a particularly effective role when it comes to instilling a common corporate culture among the executives in a company. It can become the focal point that allows groups of executives, perhaps spanning divisions and countries, to work together on issues related to common corporate values and to have the chance to expose their outcomes to the senior executives in the company. There is no doubt that the enhancement of corporate culture can be particularly well achieved through corporate universities.

The corporate university could clearly often be charged with delivering substantive executive learning. This could have to do with functional topics such as cutting-edge finance, leading marketing, extended value chain updates, organizational behavior issues and the like. While many of these programs can be "strong," there is, once again, a potential risk that they can become "inbred," at least over time. It will not be easy for the company to create a truly representative "global meeting place" in its classrooms by drawing solely on its own executives. Rather, everyone present will have similar corporate points of view. In addition, typically there will not be too much "fresh thought leadership" brought to the teaching process. Rather, there may be a tendency for the teaching to reflect "the official, best functional approach" in the given company. The result is that functional in-house executive programs offered by corporate universities can easily become rather limited and limiting.

Some corporate universities will attempt to prevent this by having faculty from various business schools and consulting firms contribute, thus allowing for more renewal when it comes to the delivery of thought leadership in the programs. Although this can clearly lead to quality improvements, there is still the issue that the outside faculty and consultants from various institutions might not be strongly coordinated and, therefore, they will not necessarily be able to deliver an integrated, research-based program. Instead, they will "teach and run." Thus, the quality of programs, delivered by a number of "cherry picked" outside teachers, will typically not match what can be delivered by business schools, where thought leadership, program design and program delivery can typically be better integrated.

All things considered, it seems safe to say that corporate universities will not replace business schools.

THE ROLE OF THE CORPORATE HUMAN RESOURCES FUNCTION

The core HR function tends to be responsible for issues relating to contractual job agreements, salaries and bonuses, individual executive assessments, performance feedback and the like. Typically, HR plays a critical role when it comes to making sure that the best talent is attracted to the company and put into the optimal jobs depending on the tasks to be carried out. Executive learning issues and the development of an explicit learning strategy are often added to HR's responsibilities nowadays. This makes sense, as it fits in logically with the annual or semi-annual performance assessments typically done for each executive, where development needs are determined based on the requirements of the job. However, as learning assumes an increasingly important role in many companies, the HR function sometimes lacks the capacity to handle the learning task on top of everything else – hence the emergence of the CLO.

THE ROLE OF THE CHIEF LEARNING OFFICER (CLO)

The CLO's mandate is often to develop a portfolio of tailored executive programs for the company. Some of these programs typically aim to instill a common corporate culture; others might have to do with addressing the learning needs that can be common to many executives. This might include upgrading particular disciplinary skills in, say, marketing, finance and the like and/or further developing the leadership capabilities of a broad set of executives – the benefit being that all would be following a consistent approach.

The CLO would thus typically work closely with the CEO and other senior line executives, as well as with the corporate HR function. CLOs also tend to be closely linked with learning communities outside their own companies, including business schools, leading consultants and/or other corporations. CLOs are, therefore, usually highly networked people, and are perhaps most effective when they sees themselves as catalysts for learning rather than keeping "control" of the learning process. There is a huge difference between being an effective catalyst and a not-so-effective learning provider-cum-gatekeeper! The ideal leader of a corporate university should probably be an informed knowledge broker, not a want-to-be professor.

Perhaps some of the most effective CLOs come from a line function and may at some point even return to a line or general management position. This experience might be useful when it comes to assessing true learning needs and priorities. It will also often make it easier for them to develop credibility in the organization. Also, the self-confidence they may have developed through success in various line functions may mean that they feel they have less to prove in terms of "showing off their own brilliance." A particularly effective approach might be to have a "rotating CLO role" to promote fresh ideas and prevent stagnation.

"CHERRY PICKING" AND PROCURING OUTSIDE LEARNING SERVICES

Executive learning – particularly if it is high quality and delivered by top business schools and/or leading consultants – might be expensive for corporations. To save funds, a corporate university or CLO might enlist the services of specific professional individuals for some parts of program delivery, i.e. as freestanding consultants, rather than negotiating with institutions such as business schools or consultants to deliver a whole program package. Often, individual faculty members can be hired privately at a lower cost than would be the case if a team of faculty were to deliver a program through a business school. Individuals do not have overheads, schools do!

The company's attempt to come up with a less expensive approach by hiring individual faculty – perhaps from different schools – might be called "cherry picking." Enlisting individual faculty for their professional insights, including their research, without compensating the business school for the investment it has made in supporting the underlying research does, however, raise several issues. While such cherry picking can clearly benefit a given company, at least in the short run, the question of who, in the end, actually funds research and pays for renewed thought leadership remains. Is it ethical for corporations to walk away from their funding responsibilities here?

In the end, many corporations recognize that such cherry picking can, broadly speaking, lead to less research-intensive knowledge in the longer term. Indeed, it can lead to a scenario that ultimately might result in the stagnation of knowledge. Consequently, many companies recognize a growing need to support research and thought leadership within business schools. They might achieve this partly by sending executives to various programs at business schools, as well as by being willing to pay more for tailored in-company programs delivered at certain business schools. They might well realize that part of the fee is indeed levied in order to cover the costs of research for faculty members, thus ensuring fresh thought leadership. And, as the following comment from Jaap de Vries, VP human resources at Borealis, shows, this type of investment can certainly pay off: "We decided to be bold and invest a lot of energy and resources into the partnership. We created an Executive Development Programme with IMD that resulted in 30 business projects. We called it Courage to Lead."[4] Some corporations may also choose to donate to a given business school to enhance its financial capacity for more research; others might sponsor endowed professorial chairs and so on.

[4] *Borealis Annual Report 2005*, www.borealisgroup.com/public/news/financial/ report_2005/print149.html (2005), accessed August 27, 2007.

A related issue is when companies entrust the corporate purchasing office with the procurement of executive programs in an attempt to keep executive education costs under control. While the focus on containing costs can typically be improved and, in some instances, legitimate cost savings can be achieved, there is nevertheless the strong potential for this to be dysfunctional. The *quality* side of the learning activities that are being procured might suffer, particularly when the professionals responsible for learning in the company are no longer centrally involved – which is typically the case. Regrettably, the procurement experts are left to negotiate with the outside providers, often settling on the cheapest of several providers. The cost side becomes dominant, usually with less concern for the educational quality side. Further, there tends to be an asymmetry in bargaining power, which potentially allows corporations to take advantage of their size relative to the size of the business school on the other side of the negotiation table. As a result, the business school may be marginalized. It may feel compelled to offer a low-priced educational initiative, realizing that it could be "this business" or "no business" at all! On a marginal cost basis, this is typically still defensible, but in the longer term, of course, sufficient resources to undertake the necessary research might disappear. Again, the quality dimension could suffer.

Outsourcing of educational activities to, say, consulting firms could also raise issues regarding the quality of learning. The particular educational needs of the firm – brought forward by its own executives – may no longer be at the forefront. Again, cost savings might come at the expense of quality in executive education. And consulting firms have their own agendas: They would clearly want to apply their own models, hence tailoring might suffer and there will always be a focus on "follow-on business." Thus, it may be difficult for a firm to disengage from the consulting firm once it has been allowed to come in. For business schools, with their focus on academic value-creation, this would (hopefully) not apply – at least not to the same extent.

SMART COMPANIES DO BOTH — OPEN ENROLLMENT AND
IN-COMPANY PROGRAMS

A.P. Moller-Maersk

Founded just over a century ago, the A.P. Moller-Maersk Group is a
worldwide organization with headquarters in Copenhagen, Denmark,
and more than 110,000 employees based in over 125 countries. In
addition to owning one of the world's largest shipping companies and
being the world leader in container-based liner shipping, it is also
involved in a wide range of activities in the energy, shipbuilding,
manufacturing and retail industries.

A.P. Moller-Maersk does not have its own physical corporate
university facilities. The executive learning is the responsibility of
the corporate HR function, not a separate CLO. The Group's CEO is
heavily involved.

Much of the learning at A.P. Moller-Maersk is related to
strengthening the competence base of individual executives. These
executives are typically sent to business schools for individual learning to develop them for the next stages in their careers and, in some
instances, to address specific functional knowledge deficiencies. The
acceleration of individuals' progress and the ability to take on more
demanding jobs are key objectives! A.P. Moller-Maersk has chosen a
relatively small number of business schools, so that there can be a
clear set of joint reference points among executives when they come
back to the sponsoring organization. Each executive goes through one
open program, chosen from a relatively small number of offerings.
Thus, while the emphasis is clearly on individual learning and
enhancing the capabilities of each executive on an individual basis,
there is also a strong corporate cultural development dimension,
stemming from the choice to focus on relatively few business schools,
and also on the enhanced corporate prestige bestowed on an executive
who is sent on one of these programs.

In addition, A.P. Moller-Maersk has embarked on an ambitious
program to enhance its competitiveness by further accelerating the
evolution of its culture and core values, as laid out by the CEO and

the senior partners. Here all of the top- to medium-level executives – around 1,000 in total – from all over the world have gone through a two-day in-company workshop with a heavy emphasis on action learning. The CEO himself has been involved in most of the programs, together with the company's four other top partners. This initiative was clearly meant to bring everyone closer together for more effective communication, to accelerate the speed of strategy implementation and to develop a more homogenous approach to organizational implementation.

Nestlé

In the space of just under 150 years, Nestlé has grown to become the world's biggest food and beverage company, with sales of CHF 98.5 billion at the end of 2006. It employs around 265,000 people worldwide and has factories or operations in almost every country.

In keeping with its philosophy of not sacrificing long-term potential for short-term performance, Nestlé has invested in a large infrastructure of in-house programs and impressive physical facilities dedicated to in-house learning. Its corporate-wide learning center, Rive-Reine, is located five minutes from the company headquarters in Vevey, Switzerland. Executives from all over the world come to Rive-Reine to attend in-house programs and to network with Nestlé's senior executives, including the CEO. In addition, there are four regional learning centers in various parts of the world. Here, too, senior line executives participate in specific program offerings.

A key benefit of this is to forge an even stronger Nestlé culture and instill common Nestlé values. Rive-Reine, along with its network of regional learning centers, has indeed become a "global meeting place," with a strong focus on bringing executives together from throughout the company. The very fact that Nestlé is so diversified, with a strong presence in every part of the world, clearly helps create this unique context. Few other companies can match this diversity in their corporate universities – they tend to be more dominated by one, or a few, country cultures. There is no doubt that the result tends to be strong buy-in to enhancing a common Nestlé corporate culture, without any country biases.

There is a full-time professional staff at Rive-Reine, typically recruited from the various functions and geographies of the company. In addition, outside professors are brought in, on a part-time basis, to bring in required competencies and to help safeguard against program deterioration through potential "inbreeding" in programs. Furthermore, in an attempt to guard against the potential dysfunctionalities and perils of cherry picking, as previously discussed, and in the quest to deliver top-quality programs consistently, Nestlé has also asked certain business schools to provide *ad hoc* in-company programs, with broad-based enrollment, say, when it wants to reinforce a particular general leadership style. Perhaps this represents a commitment to further developing the Nestlé culture by insisting that it is not linked to the internal culture of its own corporate university, but instead draws on state-of-the-art thought leadership from elsewhere.

In addition to the in-company learning activities going on in Nestlé's corporate university hierarchy, there is also a strong commitment to individual executive learning. Typically, individuals are sent to a small number of business schools, including IMD. The Program for Executive Development (PED), in particular, has virtually become a must on the CV of an executive at Nestlé who is to be promoted beyond a certain level. Individual executive development is best undertaken with executives from many companies, who learn from each other in a "global meeting place" – IMD is the hallmark of this. By consistently sending a cadre of thirty or forty executives per year to this one program, over a period of more than fifty years, Nestlé has further enhanced its corporate culture, beyond what it might have been able to achieve with a focus on its corporate university alone.

INCREMENTAL RESEARCH IS KEY

While it is clear that thought leadership needs to come from research, and that research needs to be carried out on a systematic basis in order to build on the latest thinking, it should also be clear that this does not imply a "flavor of the month" approach. Many of the issues that research deals with represent old, traditional concepts that need to be rethought and further refined. As pointed out before, the incremental nature of research is key. Leadership issues, for instance, have been at the forefront of research and business school thinking for many decades, and the present thinking, based on fresh research is perhaps not all that different from what has been pioneered before. The important point in this context is that the topics of research and teaching need not be *entirely* new, i.e. disconnected from what has been proposed in the past. Many of today's issues remain the same. What is important is that new energy and thought are applied to traditional problems and challenges. Thus, a business school should certainly not be a proponent of all new, "flavor of the month" thinking; rather, many of the issues can be better understood by applying incremental thinking, incorporating today's real world situation – a lead and be led interface between leading practitioners and researchers. Continuity in research is thus also key – in order to update one's thinking. This is more than incrementalism.

So, as we have set out to discuss in this chapter, what can the firm itself do to spearhead relevant research? In addition to being part of a cooperative partnership in research, as just outlined, the modern firm can typically also do more to specify what it sees as the relevant research agenda – what it needs from research to provide new insights to further enhance its strategic performance. How can learning partners play an action-oriented role as research partners? I see two main ways:

- Internally generated growth can take place by having more internal entrepreneurs to spearhead it. But this requires more research on how to identify new business opportunities, how to compose effective implementation teams and how to lead them. This can be best understood in the context of a specific firm where new issues come into play, such as battling a silo mentality, learning to tolerate a certain degree of "failure," having effective senior executives in place as mentors and ensuring that the CEO actively supports internally generated growth. It is easy to see that joint applied research is often necessary to develop the relevant company-specific insights and that action-learning workshops can then bring the research and learning further along.

- Keep management processes simple. As Carlos Ghosn, president and co-chairman of Nissan, says, "Simplicity requires hard work – complexity equals no work!"[5] Thus, control processes, HR processes and the like need to be better understood in this light – and this requires cooperative research and action-learning workshops. This will "push" both research insights and company-specific learning further.

Thus, we see that the corporation can, and must, do a lot when it comes to driving research – but clearly with a practical bent, related to its own strategic agenda. Often, this research becomes the client input to action-learning workshops.

IMPLICATIONS FOR LEARNING PARTNERS

1. *Executive development is a task for all:* In order to create significant value, companies need to develop along with the societies they serve. To facilitate this, a company must create a culture of ongoing learning – lifelong learning – and responsibility for this must rest with the CEO and the top management team. All layers of the company must share this corporate learning mindset – individual executives and their managers alike.

2. *Smart companies take a multidimensional approach to executive learning:* The corporate learning strategy should take into account the specific needs of the corporation – what is right for one company may not be right for the next. There are several routes

[5] C. Ghosn, Presentation given to the 5th Nikkei, Stanford and IMD Conference on Senior Leadership, Tokyo (October 24, 2005).

open to companies to help them achieve their various learning objectives:

- To relieve the HR function, a CLO can be appointed to develop a portfolio of tailored executive programs to perhaps better meet the specific learning needs of the company.
- Corporate universities can be particularly effective when it comes to instilling a common corporate culture or delivering specific substantive training and emphasizing lifelong learning. However, unless the company is a large and diverse multinational, it may be difficult to create a "global meeting place" effect in a corporate university.
- Consulting firms can be used, but it is important to keep in mind that tailoring may suffer because they tend to apply their "standard" solutions and also focus on "follow-on business."
- Learning on the job, particularly through networking and sharing best practices, will continue to be important. But when an individual executive has specific development needs, an open-enrollment program at a top business school may be the answer.
- When rapid strategic change is called for, a CEO may engage with a top business school to develop a tailored in-company program. An in-company program can accommodate a large number of executives, often working on specific assignments, in a relatively short period of time, thereby speeding up the pace of strategic change and implementation. The company must not, however, delegate full responsibility for learning to the business school. The business school can play a partnership role here – but the firm must be the key driver.

3. *Balancing cost and quality:* While it may be tempting for companies to "cherry pick" and contract with faculty privately, to save money, it is important to keep in mind that this can have a negative impact on the quality of the learning experience. In these cases, the faculty often come from different institutions and, as a result, the integration of the program design will suffer. Similarly,

some companies treat executive learning like a commodity, choosing programs purely on price. While this might serve short-term cost management needs, the real cost in the long term through lost learning and missed research opportunities will be far higher. Corporate universities, although possibly more cost effective, can lead to stagnation, especially if pressure to "fill seats" is high.

4. *Paying for research bears fruit:* Many companies value research and recognize the need to support the thought leadership that can be found within leading business schools by driving their research agendas. Companies need to beware of "flavor of the month" schools. They must keep in mind that good research is the result of an incremental process. The best concepts are developed over time, through intensive interactions with business and executives – propositional knowledge meeting prescriptive knowledge. Companies can help support research at business schools by sending executives on the various open-enrollment programs they offer, as well as by accepting to pay a premium for quality in-company programs based on fresh research.

8   Business school leadership issues

to stay on top, the school must create opportunities for its faculty to express their ideas and creativity through innovative research and educational programs . . . I would like for us to take the school to the next level and create a true community of learners where the boundaries between teacher and student start to be broken apart. In the end, the university should be a hub, or in dot-com parlance, a portal, where we bring the best of knowledge to the university and take the university's knowledge out to the world.

Patrick T. Harker, former dean, Wharton School[1]

KEY POINTS

- The three major tasks for business school leaders are: (1) being quick to identify new opportunities worth pursuing, whether in new academic areas or new geographies; (2) mobilizing the business school's resources to create academic value, i.e. through the faculty, strategic alliances with other leading business schools, and perhaps through alliances with learning partners; and (3) creating an environment of trust and inspiration, typically through a flat organization that will facilitate the necessary bonding.

- Depending on whether a business school is freestanding or part of a larger university, the leadership challenges can differ quite significantly. A freestanding business school may have fewer constraints and more control over its destiny – so it is often in a better position to seize opportunities as they arise because it has the ability to make quick decisions – but it lacks the broader knowledge base and sense of security that comes from being associated with a university.

[1] As quoted in N. Moffitt, "Meet the Dean," *Wharton Alumni Magazine* (Spring 2000), www.wharton.upenn.edu/alum_mag/issues/spring2000/feature_1.html, accessed August 27, 2007.

- Business schools with a greater orientation toward practicing managers will typically be in the freestanding category, while those with a relatively lower practitioner orientation will typically fall under the umbrella of a larger university, most often a publicly funded university.
- The top leadership role in a business school is often "temporary" in that the leader will typically go back to teaching and research or business after the term of office is over. In such cases, one can argue that the ideal term for business school leaders should be long enough to allow him or her to make an impact.
- Business school leaders need to balance their time between the classic leadership focus on top- and bottom-line performance and a broader set of objectives – social entrepreneurship – that will enhance the overall quality of management in the business school.
- As we have reinforced many times in this book, strategy means choice! But making choices often leaves some stakeholders unhappy. However, a good leader is not in the job to be popular, so popularity should not be the driver – value-creation should drive the choices.

INTRODUCTION

As Stephen Covey puts it, "Management is efficiency in climbing the ladder of success; leadership determines whether the ladder is leaning against the right wall."[2] When it comes to the leadership of a business school, we can perhaps borrow from what two well-established Dutch leaders say about their roles. Jan Aalberts, president and CEO of Aalberts Industries, an international industrial group with a leading position in the marketplace and customers that include building contractors, scientific laboratories and the telecommunications industry, says that to him leadership implies "pressure with pleasure,"[3] which

[2] S. Covey, *The 7 habits of highly effective people* (New York: Free Press, 1989).
[3] J. A. Aalberts, Presentation to IMD's Dutch Alumni 15th Anniversary Conference, Amsterdam (October 6, 2006).

underscores that while it is a demanding task, one must enjoy dealing with the challenges.

Peter Elverding, CEO of DSM, a diversified multinational manufacturing company active worldwide in nutritional and pharma ingredients, performance materials and industrial chemicals, says, "When we think we lead, we are mostly led." This implies that leadership must be rather "invisible" and that it "represents," or is mandated by, the organization that is being led. In the context of a business school, this means that the president/dean cannot be isolated from the rest of the organization. Peter Elverding also says, "A leader is a dealer in hope," which stresses another critical leadership function – the inspirational side. The key is to move the organization ahead by conveying a positive vision – a belief in the future – that is shared by all in the organization.[4]

In this chapter, I shall define what, in my opinion, makes a good business school leader, before going on to argue that it is important that business schools be given the freedom to operate on a stand-alone basis, i.e. that ideally they are not part of a larger university. I shall also discuss the three major tasks that I believe the leaders of top business schools must address in order to perform effectively: identifying new opportunities, mobilizing the business school's resources and creating trust and inspiration. Finally, I will look at leadership transition and how to go about choosing a new leader.

WHAT IS A BUSINESS SCHOOL LEADER?

It should be recognized at the outset that there are various types of organizations, and that the challenges for business school leaders will differ depending on the type of organization they are charged with leading. Clearly, the leader who runs a business school that is part of a traditional university will have a different set of tasks and challenges from the leader who runs a freestanding business school

---

[4] P. A. Elverding, Presentation to IMD's Dutch Alumni 15th Anniversary Conference, Amsterdam (October 6, 2006).

– a good leader in one environment may not be so good in another.

The leader of any business school is expected to develop an agenda of key issues that is, in essence, an extension of those of the key stakeholders – the faculty above all. The classic leadership focus on top- and bottom-line performance, just as a CEO must do, is obviously required.[5] "Clearly, a high level of financial performance creates funds for a business school dean to invest in strategic investments such as new faculty, software development and research activity."[6] However, the business school leader should also typically have a broader set of objectives – essentially, he or she must be a "social entrepreneur." These broader objectives, such as enhancing the quality of state-of-the-art management by pursuing research that contributes to a better understanding of sustainable growth, or results in more far-reaching educational programs such as special offerings to women, minorities and the like, will play important roles in creating academic value. This too is a central part of the leadership agenda for the business school leader-cum-social entrepreneur.[7]

By creating an environment that allows the classic leadership style, along with an element of social entrepreneurship, business school leaders might be able to play a truly significant and proactive role in society so that academic values can be more forward-oriented and in line with society's present and future needs. Paradoxically, perhaps, the business school leader must create this environment, this acceptance of a broader agenda. How? At IMD, for example, a research institute was created in Shanghai two years ago (as outlined earlier) to build IMD's "business" in China. But this led to a broader understanding of how to work with state-led institutions, perhaps not even following democratic ways of working, as we typically know

[5] G. Bickerstaffe, "Dean as CEO," *BizEd* (May/June, 2006), 46.
[6] H. Thomas, "Business school strategy and the metrics for success," *Journal of Management Development* 26 (2007), 32–42.
[7] D. Bernstein, *How to change the world: Social entrepreneurs and the power of new ideas* (Oxford: Oxford University Press, 2003).

them in the West. This, in turn, led to the hiring of two Chinese professors, which resulted in even more emphasis on research and marketing and, in the end, a dramatic shift in general emphasis toward Eastern thinking. The school's leadership helped create broad acceptance for this initiative!

Clearly, the top-down dimension of classic leadership is based on the leader's sense of inner drive. However, the leader must always be sensitive to and compatible with the bottom-up issues stemming from the members of the business school community. A good balance between top down and bottom up is probably important for creating better leadership in business schools. Key decisions cannot be pushed from the top alone – the faculty must want them. Equally, key decisions cannot be held up by groups of faculty alone. The process of dialoguing, give and take, listen and learn is essential – only then will a top-down/bottom-up balance emerge.

Keeping the above point on top-down/bottom-up balance firmly in mind, it is still important that business school leaders spearhead the generation of new initiatives that actually *add* value rather than spending virtually all their time and energy on day-to-day administration and maintaining the status quo. Too often, the pressure to fall into a more bureaucratic, administrative leadership role wins out. This may have to do with the fact that often there is simply not enough freedom from constraints in the business school to undertake new initiatives. The risk of this lack of freedom is that the capabilities of the business school leader might be stifled, not only when it comes to top-line and bottom-line growth but also when it comes to spearheading the more far-reaching social entrepreneurship tasks. Thus, one can perhaps see the difference between effective business school leaders who push for concrete value-creating objectives – top-line and/or bottom-line growth as well as social entrepreneurship initiatives – and those who are, in essence, glorified administrators, more or less trapped by the constraints of the institution they are set to lead.

In the context of this book, it is of course key that the business school leader has enough freedom to be able to create meaningful learning partnerships. It seems that many business schools are going through an evolutionary process whereby some of the classic constraints that were common in the past are being relaxed. For instance, firmly set, narrowly defined axiomatic departments and rigidly defined academic titles, hierarchies and tenure seem to be less of a constraint today. It is important that such evolution take place in a way that provides more "space" over time so that business school leaders feel a sense of freedom to accomplish their objectives.

While there will almost certainly always be factors constraining the top-down options for business school leaders, it is important that their institutions evolve in such a way that these constraints might become less confining over time. The business school leader's ability to build trust and present positive results may help with this evolution. But sometimes the opposite can happen – evolution could indeed lead to a further tightening of institutional constraints. Business school leaders might then feel a sense of stress because they realize that they cannot pursue their visions and objectives in such an environment. The future success of a business school may depend on institutional constraints being reduced so that there is more consistency between the top-down aspirations and the bottom-up realities

THE ARGUMENT FOR A FREESTANDING BUSINESS SCHOOL
According to Engwall, it can be useful to classify business school institutions according to higher versus lower academic orientation and higher versus lower orientation toward practitioners.[8] With a greater orientation toward practitioners, business schools are typically seen as more freestanding and perhaps "outside" a classic academic system. In contrast, with a relatively lower orientation toward practitioners, business schools might more typically be seen as belonging "inside" a classical academic institution. Engwall thus classifies university departments and university business schools,

[8] L. Engwall, Presentation at the Academy of Management Annual Meeting, Atlanta, Georgia (August 14, 2006).

which typically have relatively high academic orientations, as being "inside" the academic institution. In contrast, he sees stand-alone business schools, as well as corporate universities/consultants, as tending to have a somewhat lower academic orientation, typically "outside" the classic academic institution.

When a business school is "inside" the academic institution, Engwall sees advantages in being associated with the broader intellectual context of the university and the sense of financial stability that comes from being part of a larger entity. However, when a business school is part of a university, several more constraints will typically be "imposed" on the leader by the procedures and traditions of the broader university. These institutional constraints might result from strong bureaucratic restrictions that often include excessive processes, rules and guidelines and (overly) rigid university financial control and budgeting processes. In most cases, almost any change in programs or processes involves a slow, bureaucratic exercise where many stakeholders have the ability to slow down, or even veto the proposed change.

In contrast, the freestanding business school will not have the advantage of a broader knowledge pool, nor the financial security and academic prestige that typically come from being part of a university. However, the leader of a freestanding business school will typically have fewer institutional constraints, thus simplifying the leadership task. There is often more flexibility because the institutional rules may be less rigid, and there is a stronger possibility of being closer to the market.

In my experience, the benefits of being a freestanding business school outweigh those of being part of a classic university structure. Below, I have elaborated on the reasons for this view:

- Stand-alone business schools have more control over their resources, i.e. financial, physical facilities and others. When a business school – particularly a successful one – is part of a university, it might be tempting for the top leadership of the university to treat the school as a "cash cow." As business schools need to maintain their research focus in order to address the strong demands and needs of business today, they must have control of their own resources. Thus, there should probably be little or no room for diverting resources that have been generated by the business school to support financially less viable units elsewhere in the university.

- The more minimalist structure and processes that result from being a stand-alone school can be a real advantage. When a business school is part of a university, the burden of formal bureaucratic structures and processes can be much greater. Decision-making processes are often more cumbersome – and often more political. The speed and flexibility so critical for success in the modern business school can be lost.

- As Engwall points out, freestanding business schools typically have a higher practitioner orientation. As we have discussed, partnerships with leading corporations and executives are essential for driving the research agenda, ensuring relevance and challenging the business school to innovate – all of which are critical for meaningful academic value-creation.

Business schools that are part of a university are often pushed to support the university's objectives. For example, at the Ivey Business School, a former dean reports that the school was heavily pressured, but did not give in to:

1. Expanding the undergraduate program. A large undergraduate business program would have helped the university attract more of the best Canadian students, because the risk of not being accepted into Ivey's small (150 per year) program discouraged many good students from coming to Western. They were discouraged because Ivey only admitted business undergraduates after they had successfully completed two years of study in another part of the university. Even then, there were no guarantees because the competition to get into the program was very stiff.

2. Supporting the local business community, so they, in turn would give more financial support to the university.

IMD: A freestanding business school

IMD is a good example of a European-based business school where program fees, i.e. tuition, finance virtually all of IMD's operations. It is hard to conceive how this could be done if the business school were part of a broader university, with the temptation to use the school's financial robustness to "subsidize" other parts of the university.

Further, IMD's inner structure is rather unique – with no academic departments, no academic title hierarchy and no tenure. How could this minimalist structure be "allowed" if IMD were part of a university?

Finally, the amount of IMD's costs that are allocated to research – practical, including case research – is exceptionally high, about 27 per cent of overall operating costs. It is hard to see how this high commitment level could be maintained if IMD were part of a university, with the typical levying of "overhead taxes" that universities impose on their operating units.

THE FOUNDATION OF SUCCESSFUL LEADERSHIP – DISCRETIONARY RESOURCES

Effective business school leadership has a lot to do with how to create sufficient resources in order to generate the freedom to maneuver the business school and pursue new academic initiatives with longer-term payoffs – both traditional and social entrepreneurship initiatives. To create these discretionary resources, a clear focus on both the bottom line and the top line are necessary. It is also important to be realistic when going after academic initiatives. Thus, it is perhaps a good idea for a business school to be "run like a business," i.e. with a clear focus on pursuing segments within the academic field that indeed offer the potential for growth and for yielding net profits.

Many business schools rely, to a greater or lesser extent, on outside funding, say, from a university and/or the public sector. The "problem" with public sources of funding, however, is that they often bring with them strong stakeholder constraints. Thus, the business school may end up having public sector figures as part of its governance. There will often be excessively constraining control processes, which might lead to more bureaucracy rather than creativity. An illustrative point here is the amount of bureaucracy associated with new research proposals funded by the European Community, the so-called Amadeus process.[9] When funding is finally made available, typically after spending a huge amount of intellectual energy on putting the proposal together, the next step for the business school is to be open to "auditors" from Brussels. The auditors will then pursue a rather bureaucratic control process, which is also time- and energy-consuming for those involved. In the end, there may not be much time and energy left to do the research! It is indeed difficult to see how academic value-creation can effectively take place with such an overly bureaucratic process.

Business schools, of course, should typically be not-for-profit organizations. Clearly, there is little room for profit maximization *per se*, if this is meant to lead to paying dividends to outside shareholders. However, as noted, this does not mean that the business school should not be run like a profit-seeking organization. The additional resources allow more flexibility to go after new opportunities. When the economic results are good, they also allow for the payment of bonuses for good performance (in teaching and research) to inside stakeholders, professors above all!

It goes without saying that an organization, even though it is not-for-profit, must still have clear organizational procedures, clear budgets, clear guidelines regarding cost containment – clear control

[9] Amadeus is an ESPRIT (European Strategic Programme for Research and Development in Information Technology) project on a multi-method approach to the development of universal specifications. www.uta.fi/FAST/GC/eurgloss.html (accessed 27 September 2006).

processes – so that resources are not spent in a wasteful manner. This also means that the business school leader must be consistent and strict when it comes to the implementation of these guidelines – no different rules for different constituencies, no "side deals!" Thus, full transparency will be a critical part of good business school leadership. The integrity of the leadership function must be beyond doubt.

Once the foundation for leading has been established, there are three major sets of tasks that the leaders of top business schools must address in order to perform effectively. These are addressed in the following sections.[10]

Leadership task no. 1: See new opportunities before everyone else

The business school leader-cum-entrepreneur must be able to *see* academic value-creating opportunities before they are obvious to everyone else. The ability to articulate a new business idea early on seems critical to enhance cutting-edge leadership and academic value-creation. In order to do this, it is vital for the business school leader to have a clear understanding of the environment, the marketplace, developments at other competitive business schools and in academia at large, and the like. The leader can facilitate this by developing a good network of professors and other thought leaders within academia. A similar network with practitioners is also necessary to sense the cutting-edge issues businesses are currently facing. We have referred to this as a clear outside-in, market-driven focus, and I have discussed it extensively earlier in the book, implying that strong business school leadership has to do with having an articulate, outside-in vision regarding the key tasks to be done.

Of course, an ability to see opportunities which are not obvious to everyone else would also require a reasonable amount of freedom to operate, think and act more broadly, and not to be too limited by

---

[10] B. Chakravarthy and P. Lorange, *Profit or growth? Why you don't have to choose* (Philadelphia, PA: Wharton/Pearson, 2007).

the formal constraints and guidelines that are often present in academic institutions. The classic views of stakeholders in traditional academic settings, such as the professors and staff, and perhaps even the politicians who fund the academic institutions, could easily discourage opportunity seeking in the initial phase. Thus, in order to see new academic value-creating opportunities more clearly, there has to be a certain degree of freedom to think openly and a strong element of space for new initiatives. However, if there is the perception that the stakeholders have too much control, this might discourage the business school leader from pursuing new opportunities – a "there is no point" attitude may develop.

The ability to see potential opportunities in the various market segments that the business school typically serves is particularly critical. For example, there has been no growth in the classic MBA segment for several years. As already mentioned, from 2003 to 2005, for instance, the number of new students taking the GMAT test has dropped, an indication that the MBA market might be stagnant or even shrinking. Recent statistics for 2006, however, might point toward a turnaround in this market.[11] The Executive MBA market, on the other hand, has generally been seen to be slightly more robust and so perhaps offers more opportunities. It is worth reinforcing here that even though the commercial rationale for offering a strong MBA program might be questionable, there is no doubt that from an intellectual point of view a good MBA program can be essential. Cutting-edge research can find its way to the MBA classroom relatively easily, and new program development can flourish. I would say that at IMD our small, elite MBA program is our most important one when it comes to academic value-creation, although commercially it certainly is not!

The Ph.D. market might also be a constraint in the sense that it typically requires large amounts of resources to run a good quality

---

[11] T. Pepper, "Crunch this: B-schools rebound from an identity crisis," *Newsweek International Edition* (August 21, 2006), msnbc.msn.com/id/14325067/, accessed August 30, 2007.

PhD program. Above all, the faculty resource needs are significant, and the cost of running a first-class PhD program may simply be too high to be a reasonable opportunity for many business schools. However, for schools without a PhD program to support their academic value-creation, there is still an option available. Outstanding graduates/candidates from *other* schools' PhD programs can be hired to support faculty in their research, in the academic "legwork." In this way, only proven talents are employed, with little waste of faculty energy on supervising average-to-mediocre candidates in a school's own PhD program.

Undergraduate business education may not be very attractive in a commercial or academic value-creation sense. Admittedly, a heavy teaching focus here might open up sources of relatively easy funding, particularly when doctoral candidates are employed as teachers and outside lecturers are extensively employed. But there is a lot of competition, including non-business faculties in other academic institutions. And the potential for the faculty to actually learn much or stimulate their research may be less prevalent. Thus, it would be hard to see a platform for extensive growth here.

To repeat one of the main messages of this book, one area that has real growth potential, however, is the executive education field. There seems to be a clear need in the marketplace for tailored, in-company programs. Similarly, there seems to be growth potential for open-enrollment programs. And, importantly, the potential for faculty learning – lead and be led – is there! Thus, from the viewpoint of a business school leader, it seems important to be able to see new opportunities within the executive education arena, and to stimulate the business school to pursue these opportunities.

From a geographic point of view, it could perhaps be argued that new opportunities might be expected to come from those parts of the world where there is the highest potential for long-term growth, and where the population is perhaps large enough to offer the potential to attract many new students/clients. China and India, in particular, would represent such opportunities. The business school leader needs to stimulate the business school to go after emerging academic opportunities in such promising new geographies in a realistic way.

Thus, as we have already noted, IMD has a research center in Shanghai, which has already led to significantly more research on Chinese business practices that can be of value to participants from all over the world, including Chinese participants who can get a better feel – in the global meeting place – for how other nationalities react to these findings. Another research center in Mumbai, similarly has led to more India-in-the-world-based research. Both of these activities have led to stronger academic value-creation at IMD in Lausanne, as executives from all over the world are exposed to the new insights coming from these two centers. It also means that IMD might be able to spearhead further thought leadership for a better worldwide understanding of Asian insights. And, as mentioned, it goes both ways! Broad interaction with leaders from all over the world might also directly benefit Chinese and Indian leaders.

Mintzberg sees the leadership challenge to search for new opportunities as being based on *insight*. This would be based on a combination of "art," i.e. a creative mind, of "craft," i.e. of understanding the leadership craft required to run business schools, and of "science," i.e. of having a good academic grounding regarding what is going on in the field. Mintzberg does not see this as representing intellectual rigor, *per se*, or intellectual relevance either. Instead, he thinks that the business school leader and the executives involved in the academic value-creating process must be able to interface with, to be comfortable with, all three dimensions – art, craft and science – and that this creates academic value.[12] This is another way of saying that the effective business school leader must have a balanced outlook!

---

[12] H. Mintzberg, *Managers, not MBAs: A hard look at the soft practice of managing and management development* (San Francisco, CA: Berrett-Koehler Publishers, 2004).

Leadership task no. 2: Identify and mobilize the relevant resources

A business school leader must be able to identify and mobilize the resources and competencies needed to go after new initiatives in such a way that positive academic value is created. Academic value would include research outputs, delivery of educational programs, development of learning partnerships and the like. Clearly, there might be professors within the business school who might be eager – and who have the competencies – to go after new opportunities. A good business school leader should stimulate, to the highest degree, initiatives from professors to which they can apply their competencies. It is better and almost always more meaningful to say "yes" to new initiatives more often than to say "no."

At the same time, the leader must be keenly aware of critical constraints when it comes to how far it is possible to push the business school. This requires an overall mission and a disciplined and focused approach from the top so that one does not end up with an excessively diversified portfolio of initiatives. At IMD, for instance, the vision is rather tight and the focus is rather clear. Within this framework, however, there is still plenty of room for initiatives by individual professors. Strategy means choice – otherwise the school will not get to where it wants to be. The most severe bottleneck might be to identify and attract suitable professors. This requires flexible and adaptive hiring practices.

Above all, an effective faculty member must be active on the research front, indeed, so that he or she is working on cutting-edge dilemmas. Typically, he or she will be operating within a cross-cultural reality and realize that there are more dilemmas than finite answers. Thought leadership is the key.

As we have stressed, it is perhaps equally important that faculty members bring their research to the classroom quickly for dialogue with a cross-section of leading practitioners. The propositional inputs from research must meet the prescriptive inputs from leading practitioners. We have also seen that it is a matter of learning for everyone – professors and participants alike. Professors, therefore, must have the ability to put themselves in the participants' shoes, so that they can listen and learn – just as much as they give. This open-minded style is vital.

Furthermore, it might be desirable for faculty members to be comfortable with working in networks, i.e. on team-based projects, when it comes to both research and teaching. They would also need to be effective in small groups, discussing research and/or pedagogical issues with colleagues and participants on an ongoing basis. This might be in contrast to some academics, perhaps in more traditional academic settings, where the research that they are working on is at times "kept under wraps," only to be published when it is finally finished. In my opinion, good research progress depends on constant interaction with colleagues and learning partners.

Another characteristic of an effective faculty member, therefore, is that he or she is also comfortable with team-based publishing and equally at ease with getting feedback and incentives based on these team-based efforts. Again, we can at times see a contrast here with academics in some classic academic settings, where in essence only single-author publications count for academic merit. My view would be exactly the opposite: The fact that two or more faculty members can work together effectively is an excellent expression of demonstrated strength for all.

There will also be opportunities to add new intellectual resources to the business school, via both focused research and new hiring. Ideally, new hiring should take place in such a way that the overall quality of the business school is increased by each new hire. In other words, the importance of strong intellectual insights, a strong ability to exercise thought leadership, must not be underestimated. And good academic talent tends to create its own demand. Contrary to what is typically taught in economics, one could say, "supply creates its own demand."[13]

[13] J. B. Say, *A Treatise on Political Economy* (Philadelphia, PA: Lippincott, Grambo & Co. 1855, trans. C. R. Prinsep, ed. Clement C. Biddle, 1855), www.econlib.org/library/Say/sayT1.html, accessed September 22, 2006.

There can also be productive links with academics outside of one's own school. This could be in visiting professorships and visiting lecturers. With other academic institutions, there can also be joint teaching and/or research programs. As already mentioned in Chapter 3, IMD has three active academic links, with the Sloan School of Management at MIT and the two Swiss Federal Institutes of Technology – ETH in Zurich and EPFL in Lausanne.

Why not "bring the best together," through joint ventures with other academics and/or institutions, in general, for a broader set of programs and initiatives? It is interesting to see that, from an economic standpoint, strategic alliances do not necessarily create clear top line and/or bottom line results, and they can also require extraordinary amounts of time and energy. Strong financial results are perhaps typically more easily created when the business school is 100 per cent in charge of its own resources. Thus, strategic alliances should perhaps take place primarily when it is not feasible for the business school on its own to attain the unique academic value within a specific field, and when it would be advantageous to mobilize the broader academic prestige that comes from a joint venture. Perhaps the most important "alliances," therefore, would be with various business organizations-cum-learning partners. Through these learning partnerships, the lead and be led effect can come into full play, thus stimulating and further developing the knowledge base of the business school's faculty. By learning from the best of practice, the faculty will gain incremental knowledge benefits for the various research initiatives that they are pursuing.

Leadership task no. 3: Be an inspirational leader

Business school leaders need to be inspirational leaders, in the sense that they are ideally part of a flat organization, preferably without much hierarchy or silos, so that all professors are "colleagues." Ideally, there needs to be a strong focus on a participatory organizational process, rather than a heavily institutionalized bureaucratic one. Many committees and interminable meetings should be avoided!

Unfortunately, many business schools have organizational structures that make inspirational leadership difficult. Many schools, for instance, are organized according to academic departments, with strong processes for promotion and tenure that may make it difficult for the business school leader to inspire new value-creation by the team. The business school leader may have difficulty having an impact on tenured professors in well-defined disciplinary fields who "rule" their kingdoms.

Bonding with professors is thus critical.[14] Good business school leaders should be in their positions because the faculty and, to some extent, the other stakeholders want them to be there to carry out the leadership tasks on their behalf. Thus, a sense of trust and bonding will be important. If stakeholders see business school leaders as pursuing their own agenda and aspirations too much, say for their next career step, rather than doing what is seen to be best for the business school, it can be difficult to see how trust and bonding can be maintained. In this sense, the business school leader is clearly much more of a temporary leader than you would find in a typical private organization. When their term is over, business school leaders usually return to being regular professors.

THE ROLE OF THE BOARD

In a well-functioning governance process of a business school, there will be important complementary roles to be held by the board, with its chair, the dean/president with his/her administration. The board normally will have four broad areas of function:

1. To review and monitor the financial resource side of the school, including the approval of proposed budgets, overall performance assessments and decisions on major uses of resources, such as for research, infrastructure (say to IT), buildings, maintenance programs, etc.

---

[14] G. Kohlrieser, *Hostage at the table: How leaders can overcome conflict, influence others, and raise performance* (San Francisco, CA: Jossey-Bass Publishers, 2006).

2. Monitoring the general progress of the school, such as when it comes to programs for faculty hiring and development, marketing programs for various revenue generating activities – including reviewing the balance when it comes to sources of revenue including geographic mix.

3. Managing the search and selection for a new dean or president. The issue of leadership succession is key – or course. We have seen throughout this book that the top leadership tasks in a modern business school are complex and formidable. The key, of course, is to approach succession in such a way that new ideas and thinking can be added – new leadership represents a great opportunity for this! At the same time, there should not be too much room for taking excessive risk re the new leader's competence profile – he or she should have a well-proven track record. And, of course, the growth potential of the individual chosen is also key – and probably hardest to assess!

4. There is one further and difficult task for which the board is responsible – namely to intervene in case of unsatisfactory performance by the dean/president, and possibly remove him or her. Performance review sessions – systematic and on an annual/semi-annual basis – will be key so that expectations are clear. Situations leading to dismissal can tend to be disruptive – and dysfunctional – of course. Clearly one should attempt to avoid this!

CHOICE OF THE BUSINESS SCHOOL LEADER

We have already alluded to the fact that the choice of the business school leader must be acceptable to a broad set of stakeholders, above all the professors, so that the initial conditions for trust building and bonding are present. I have also alluded to the fact that the business school leader must have a clear sense of mission, indeed a profile that demonstrates this, as well as a demonstrated unselfishness and willingness to give all his or her energy to the leadership task. In many ways, the business school leader would be, in a sense, similar to a leader of an ideal organization – with full, idealistic commitment.

How are these business school leaders chosen? In some business schools, there is an election process, which, above all, can ensure that the internal stakeholders get their views properly represented. However, such processes can also lead to the *de facto* choice of rather weak leaders, in the sense that it might be hard for broader coalitions of professors to agree on prospective candidates *per se*. Paradoxically, it might be easier for more nondescript candidates to be elected! Therefore, there has been a trend in recent years to have a search committee appoint a new business school leader. Search committees can perhaps be more proactive in coming up with a desired profile of the business school leader that might be needed at a particular point in time. This may be in contrast to the elected leader, who might possibly have a profile more consistent with traditions of the past, rather than with the needs of the future.

It is typically desirable that there is a good overlap and mutual respect (even if the new leader will take the school in a somewhat different direction) between the outgoing and the incoming president/dean so that the transfer of relationships with learning partner firms throughout the world can take place seamlessly. Other important network contacts would be the alumni, as well as the foundation board and the executive committee (IMD-specific) or advisory committee (more general label).

It is important that the outgoing president/dean does not influence or interfere directly in the choice of the successor, nor attempt to interfere with the strategies that are set and pursued after he or she steps down. This might perhaps be in contrast with the typical management succession planning in large business organizations, where the outgoing CEO is often expected to play a major role when it comes to grooming and choosing a successor, who will continue with the existing strategies – at least for a while.

While there are variations in models from school to school, it seems important to me that the president/dean be given enough time in office to have an impact. Today, with presidents/deans usually having relatively short tenures, there may not be enough opportunity for continuity and the resulting long-term impact from the top. Conversely, having the president/dean stay in office too long might mean that he or she becomes overly conservative and less dynamic over the years. Risk aversion and a tendency "not to rock the boat" might set in. The need for a balance is well stated by Edward A. Snyder, dean of the Graduate School of Business at the University of Chicago, who says, "Deans who want to stay a long time can become too timid, and that's not good. On the other hand, if your stay is too short, you may become reckless."[15] According to Fee and colleagues, the mean dean tenure for the top twenty-five MBA schools from 1996 to 2002 was 4.372 years.[16] In my view, the minimum time needed might be at least five years plus whatever time is required to find and put the next dean in place – during this period, the existing dean essentially becomes a lame duck. Obviously, this depends on the degree of change required and how freestanding the school is.

In most organizations, a major task of top management is to prepare the next generation of leaders. Would this be the case for business schools too, or are all responsibilities for the choice of a new leader, and an orderly transition process, essentially in the hands of the search committee? In my view, business schools are different from most other organizations in that the search committee (appropriately) plays such a dominant, critical role. Still the incumbent leadership team of a school can facilitate a better transition, by sharing critical tasks with other faculty members, who thus can "learn" the many details involved in leading the school. These faculty members – who may be considered as back-ups to the present top management – may or may not be asked to play roles as part of the incoming management team.

---

[15] Bickerstaffe, "Dean as CEO," 46.

[16] C. E. Fee, C. J. Hadlock and J. R. Pierce, "Business school rankings and business school deans: A study of nonprofit governance," www.aacsb.edu/Resource_Centers/ Rankings/FMA-BusinessSchoolRankings.pdf, accessed November 6, 2007.

IMD's leadership transition process

At IMD, there is a search committee consisting of three members of IMD's executive committee of the foundation board – senior corporate practitioners – and three elected members from IMD's professorial staff. The chairman of the search committee is also the chairman of the IMD executive committee of the foundation board, i.e. an outside executive. He has a double vote, in case of a tie in the votes of the six search committee members.

The committee operates under total secrecy and confidentiality. IMD's entire foundation board must confirm its final choice. This board consists of forty-five leading executives. A confirmation by the professors is not necessary. Still, it goes without saying that, in order to be effective, a business school leader must have the broad acceptance of the professors at IMD. Hopefully, this can be achieved via the inputs from the three academic members of the search committee. The conditions for bonding and trust building must be there – the professors must consider the chosen leader as one that they actually *want* to represent them.

The search committee has focused on the following eight criteria in the selection of a new dean/president. He or she:

1. Must have demonstrated a practical approach to thought leadership.
2. Must be comfortable with the way IMD approaches academic value-creation, i.e. with "real world, real learning" and "the global meeting place."
3. Must be able to network effectively with IMD's external stakeholders, above all for program marketing and for fundraising, especially with:
    - Companies, including the Learning Network
    - Individuals, including alumni.
4. Must be able to work effectively with IMD's faculty, above all on:

- Recruitment
- Faculty reviews; contract renewals.

5. Must be able to lead the administration of IMD.
6. Must have demonstrated, through earlier jobs, that he or she:
   - Has inspirational leadership capabilities
   - Is willing/able to mobilize full energy/commitment to the task
   - Has a non-political style, with no "side deals"
   - Has a high level of personal integrity.
7. Must have a particular aptitude for continuing IMD's emphasis on executive programs, rather than on the more classic academic programs.
8. Must have considerable outside visibility and status, commensurate with IMD's strong worldwide position.

Transition team

At IMD, a transition team of four, consisting of the current president and senior associate dean and two faculty members was established approximately a year and a half before the current administration's departure. Two younger faculty members are shadowing the president and senior associate dean in order to get essential insights regarding their tasks. In addition, regularly scheduled meetings are being held, where many extensive issues are being discussed. Thus, the two new faculty members will get better insights regarding key managerial dilemmas. The new administration can then tap into this depository of knowledge as it might wish.

While an approach with a transition team seems to work well, it should not be hidden that this is also time-consuming, and with the inherent danger that decision-making might be slowed down. The clarity, in terms of "who is responsible for what" may also potentially become blurred.

IMPLICATIONS FOR BUSINESS SCHOOLS

- A business school leader must be able to identify and have the freedom to pursue a new generation of value-creating initiatives. In order to pursue these new initiatives, he or she must be realistic about the available resources, including the competency base of the institution. There will always be constraints in academia, and the effective business school leader needs to recognize them and deal with them – not be limited by them. A focus on academic initiatives where there is strong growth and profit potential will provide the discretionary resources required for long-term sustainability. The ability to mobilize the necessary "competencies" will also be necessary.
- It is critical that the business school leader has a disciplined, focused approach and clear mission so that the portfolio of initiatives does not become overly diversified. Strategy means choice! Focus is all!
- In addition to top-line and bottom-line growth, an effective business leader will also be committed to a broader set of objectives – social entrepreneurship – a true commitment to advancing the field of business in this broad sense.
- While I have put forward the merits of a stand-alone business school, the effective business school leader – regardless of the type of organization – must undertake the leadership challenge on behalf of the faculty and other key stakeholders. This will facilitate the creation of the bonding and trust that are required to be an inspirational leader – that is, someone with a clear mission who relies on inspiration to lead rather than hierarchy, seniority and titles.
- When searching for a business school leader it is important to recognize that there are various types of organizations each with its own set of unique challenges and each calling for different types of leaders.
- It is better to have a small search committee, representative of the key stakeholders, come up with the profile of the business school

leader that is required at a particular point in time. Business school leaders who are elected tend to have a profile that is more consistent with the past than with the future needs of the school. It can also typically be difficult to gain consensus, so there is more chance of getting a "safe, but mediocre" leader.

9 Conclusion: So, what are the key success factors?

> The key ingredients to be a world-class institution are: (1) faculty commitment to research and teaching excellence, not one or the other; (2) a committed professional staff who understand higher education; (3) quality of students admitted; (4) financial resources; and (5) leadership of the dean/director. If any one of these is missing, becoming a recognized world-class institution is not in the cards.
>
> F. D. S. Choi, emeritus dean, Stern School of Business[1]

KEY POINTS

- There is no "one size fits all" model for business schools, as the various successful schools around the world, each with a different model, show. But a business school strategy needs to be unique in order to create value and competitive advantage.
- Research-based thought leadership is essential for success, but it must be based on practical research – and brought to the classroom fast! Therefore, a heavy allocation of resources to research is a key factor in ensuring that the school stays at the forefront of practical thought leadership.
- An outstanding faculty is equally critical – they must be intellectual leaders who have the ability to work *with* leading businesses, to listen, to give and take, to lead and be led! Intellectual curiosity, a sense of modesty and a commitment to eclectic research are all essential.
- There must be focus and a strong economic rationale for which programs to pursue – strategy means choice. The programs must be in segments that have strong growth and the learning partners should have the capability to pay for this – based on top quality, of

---

[1] P. Lal Joshi, "India's top-ranking B-schools are at a crossroads," *Worldpress.org* (May 12, 2006), www.worldpress.org/Asia/2346.cfm, accessed August 30, 2007.

course. In the end, a school should be prepared to be financially self-sufficient, based solely on the support it receives from its learning partners. And, of course, none of these partners should be dominant.

- The successful culture of the school encompasses speed, dynamism and freedom for all to "when in doubt do the right thing!" Excessive committee work only consumes faculty time and easily leads to discouragement and even politicking. A minimalist approach is key.
- The school needs a strong leader – dean or president. Clearly, the business school leader must be highly sensitive to the preferences of the faculty; after all, it is the mandate from the faculty that makes a business school leader succeed. At the same time, the business school leader must not be afraid and must be entirely fair in applying policies and guidelines – no biases and no "side deals." The dean or president must always be seen to act in the best interests of the school.
- Transparency is also a key success factor: Workload, salaries (within bands), sabbaticals and the like must be publicly available to all faculty members – again, fairness must prevail.

CULTURE, REPUTATION, RANKINGS AND STRATEGIC CHOICES

In his path-breaking doctoral thesis, Shlomo Ben-Hur studied the relationship between the culture and performance of European business schools.[2] Interestingly, in his analysis he describes the history of business schools as a "series of pendulum swings." The academic versus the professional dimension seems to be driving the amplitude of the pendulum. He cites Cheit's model of 1985, which calls for a minimum level of academic excellence for a business school to be viable.[3] He also

---

[2] S. Ben-Hur, "Culture and performance of European business schools," Doctoral thesis, Humboldt-Universität, Berlin (2006).

[3] E. F. Cheit, "Business schools and their critics," *California Management Review* 27 (1985), 43–62.

cites the work by Cotton and colleagues, which calls not only for a minimum level of academic excellence but also for a minimum level of professional performance within the school – both need to be present for the business school to be viable.[4] In other words, there would clearly be minimum hurdles to overcome or requirements to meet for a business school to qualify as a "good" school.

Ben-Hur then stresses that the business school today faces many more challenges than before. These include globalization, changes in technology, the rise in the presence and prominence of corporate universities, changes in funding, changes in the autonomy of business schools, additional requirements when it comes to marketing and branding, and the like. He claims that this calls for a revised, more focused strategy on the part of the business school.

Specifically, Ben-Hur also claims that culture influences performance and that business schools should, therefore, review their culture and exploit the performance improvement potential available to them by strengthening aspects of their culture. There are external aspects of culture, such as sense of mission and adaptability, which he finds have a particular influence on external aspects of performance, such as financial viability, citizenship and the like. Similarly, there are internal aspects of culture, such as capacity development and consistency variables, which he claims can have a particular influence on the internal aspects of performance, such as program quality. Ben-Hur thereby reaches the conclusion that a business school should come up with differentiated strategies that translate into success in corresponding performance areas, with a relative focus on the external or internal aspects of culture depending on the particular needs of the school. Clear strategic choices are necessary.

Interestingly, Ben-Hur then indicates that quality-rating systems

---

[4] C. C. Cotton, J. F. McKenna, S. Van Auker and M. L. Meuter, "Action and reaction in the evolution of business school missions," *Management Decision* 39 (2001), 227–233.

such as EQUIS (perhaps the leading international system of quality assessment, improvement and accreditation of higher education institutions in management and business administration) tend to develop more of an internal focus on quality. By contrast, external rankings, such as those published by the *Financial Times*, *Business Week* and The Economist Intelligence Unit (see Appendix I), tend to focus more on external success as seen by the market. Again, there is a strong link between culture and overall performance, but some cultural dimensions can lead to a strengthening of the internal side of performance whereas other cultural variables can lead to a strengthening of the external side of performance.

As Wedlin notes, rankings may have tended to reinforce the preference for the typical American business school model, i e. as the "best organizational form" for delivering high quality management education.[5] This is perhaps most accentuated by the rankings undertaken by the *Financial Times* or the Economist Intelligence Unit, which try to develop measurable criteria for the academic value-creating process. A heavy focus on axiomatic dimensions tends to dominate such ratings, particularly when it comes to ranking research output, which is typically measured by publications in classic axiomatic journals. Little or no consideration would be given to emerging eclectic research. Typically, one can thus say that these types of rankings are biased toward the traditional business school, and consequently do not necessarily treat business schools that follow other academic value-creating models fairly, i.e. business schools that focus on eclecticism and non-classical structures. As Bennis and O'Toole note, many business schools today go wrong by focusing on research that is too narrow and esoteric rather than research that is of practical relevance to business.[6]

However, there are other rankings that tend to rely more

[5] L. Wedlin, "Playing the ranking game: Field formation and boundary-work in European management education," Doctoral thesis, Uppsala, Uppsala University (2004).

[6] W. G. Bennis and J. O'Toole, "How business schools lost their way," *Harvard Business Review* 83 (May 2005), 96–104.

heavily on perceived reputation by the marketplace, such as the opinions of recruiters, business school deans and students. Rankings by *Business Week* and the *Wall Street Journal* would fall into this category. Reputation seems to be increasingly important. As Engwall put it, "Reputation, therefore, is a crucial factor in the selection of a particular education."[7] However, some argue that reputation can perhaps be a distorting factor when it comes to selecting a business school. According to Crainer and Dearlove, "Business schools are just mechanisms to select elites ... People don't go to top business schools just for the learning; they go to join an elitist club, which has little to do with their ability as managers."[8] Thus choosing a business school based on reputation is, of course, no guarantee that the quality of the learning will live up to expectations.

One can perhaps argue, as Engwall has, that what has so far been the exclusivity dimension of top academic education generally might decline, as the number of players in the field increases. "Therefore the [rating-based] reputation of the institution will be even more significant in the future."[9]

IMD is now ranked consistently among the top business schools in the world (see Appendix I for a summary of some of these rankings). To some degree, IMD's generally strong rankings validate its efforts to deliver the very best executive development programs to executives from all over the world.

But rankings come and go. And there can always be honest disagreements about how specific phenomena are measured, how the various factors are ranked together and the like. It would be good if the criteria behind a specific ranking were clear, and if various weightings for different variables apply, these should also be transparent. But, as I often say, "One person might prefer a yellow apple, another a green apple, a third a red apple – and all three are,

[7] L. Engwall, "The anatomy of management education," *Scandinavian Journal of Management* 23 (March 2007), 4–35.

[8] S. Crainer and D. Dearlove, *Gravy training: Inside the business of business schools* (San Francisco, CA: Jossey-Bass, 1999), 105.

[9] Engwall, "The anatomy of management education," 4–35.

of course, right!" In other words, the market is segmented – not all customers are seeking the same experience. It is important, therefore, that the rankings should *not* drive the school's strategy. Consequently, at IMD, we hope to attribute our seeming progress to some other factors. Many of these have been reflected so far in this book. Key among them is the research-based pedagogical delivery by all – where every professor follows the lead and be led value-creating approach of propositional knowledge (from research) *always* meeting prescriptive knowledge (from practice). Although necessary, these are not sufficient conditions to explain IMD's progress. Let us, in the following paragraphs, highlight a few other key factors.

MARKET ACCEPTANCE OF IMD'S SERVICES

Perhaps a more meaningful way to look at a business school's performance would be to examine its revenue-generating capabilities to get an indication of how well the market actually accepts and appreciates the services of the school. Figure 9.1 indicates the development of revenue generation at IMD. Since IMD was founded in 1990, as a result of the merger between two smaller business schools – IMEDE in Lausanne and IMI in Geneva – the results have been impressive. Particularly in the last six to eight years, it seems clear that IMD has had a strong group of followers in the marketplace when it comes to learning partnerships with executives and firms alike.

One can, of course, ask whether this growth in revenue is a result of an increase in the faculty and staff size or, more fundamentally, whether it comes from value-based growth. The latter is true. Figure 9.1 also indicates the size of the faculty at IMD since 1992. As one can see, the faculty size has remained remarkably stable for the most part. Most of the growth, therefore, has to do with IMD being able to offer new programs with higher market value and, accordingly, a higher price. This "endorsement from the market" can perhaps, above all, be seen as an indication of the relevance of IMD's offerings and can, indeed, explain its strong performance.

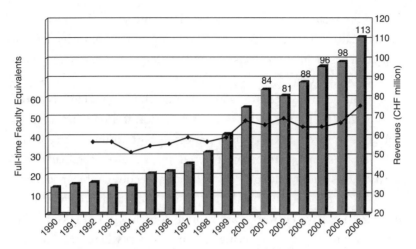

FIGURE 9.1 Evolution of IMD's revenue and faculty.

It is also apparent from Figure 9.1 that IMD is a relatively small school, and always has been. It is interesting to note that, even though the school is small, certainly relative to all of its main competitors, it is still able to be highly competitive – by offering top-quality programs in a boutique/elite context. One might note that the faculty has grown by 50 per cent while revenue has grown seven times. Expectations are high, so everything we do – from teaching, to the facilities, to creating marketing materials, to support, to catering has to be consistently of "Rolex" quality. IMD's strong position, year after year, in the various rankings of leading business schools certainly testifies to this.

ENTREPRENEURIAL LEADERSHIP

There is a strong entrepreneurial spirit at IMD that has contributed significantly to the school's success. Often in academia, there can be endless debate about what direction to take. This can sometimes result in missed opportunities. The team at IMD prefers to run the institute more like a business, which also means that we are interested in our bottom line. A strong bottom line means more funds for faculty remuneration, the ability to maintain a reasonable teaching load, more focus on research, new buildings and so on. As a result, we have tried to turn our backs on bureaucracy and chosen a leadership approach based on quick decisions and implementation to allow us to seize opportunities.

This certainly requires a clear top-down vision. I feel, as noted before, that there is a real risk of dysfunction if a one-dimensional bottom-up process takes over. A top-down/bottom-up balance is the key. It takes energy from the top, all the time, to achieve this – without this energy, the process will easily become unbalanced, and might even die out. It is analogous to the second law of thermodynamics – negative entropy. For example, a rock will fall if you lift it up and then let it go, hot frying pans cool down when taken off the stove, air in a high-pressure tire shoots out from even a small hole in its side to the lower pressure atmosphere. In each of these examples, energy of some kind is changing from being localized ("concentrated" in the rock or the pan) to becoming more spread out. The same can be applied to business schools – the energy must always be injected by the leadership of the school; if it is unilaterally dispersed among the members of the organization, then there will potentially be a tendency to settle for the status quo – negative entropy. The second law of thermodynamics does indeed apply – energy must be put in from the top.

The role of the president at IMD

The president's role at IMD is strong for various reasons. It is felt that clarity from the top is important, in order to enhance strong execution and the speedy and flexible setting of direction. Consistency and focus are perhaps key words here; strong inputs from the top are necessary for this.

Much of the rationale for the strong role of the president is that it is also intended to preserve faculty energy, so that the faculty can avoid getting bogged down in committees, managing staff and spending endless amounts of time on various tasks to do with evaluation/promotion, so typical in many business schools. These activities tend simply to swallow time and energy, detracting from research and innovative teaching. For these reasons, the president is also centrally involved when it comes to faculty hiring decisions as well as contract reviews and renewals.

FOCUSED STRATEGY

Strategy means choice! There are so many different directions that a business school could potentially follow. A clear focus seems paramount, i.e. to choose a destiny and develop a consistent, simple strategy that will enable the school to stay focused and through this create strong academic value. Too often, there are examples of business schools that choose highly complex strategies, perhaps based on the idea of "letting all the flowers bloom!" In my experience, centrifugal forces then easily set in, and the academic value-creating process suffers. Over the years, I have come to believe that business schools, with their faculty who should be specialists on strategic management, *de facto* can only handle very simple, robust strategies – only then can all understand and buy in.

Above all, a strategy must have a unique value proposition, compared to the strategies of competitors. At IMD, we view this as having a strong "investment" in new thoughts, new conceptual thinking as well as a strong commitment to bringing this new thinking into the classroom fast. The uniqueness of IMD's strategy includes a practical, hands-on focus on new knowledge discovery (research) *and* a primary focus on executive education in the "global meeting place."

As noted, our MBA program is not large, but rather small and elite; we have neither an undergraduate program nor a PhD program; and we do not have campuses in geographic locations other than Lausanne, Switzerland. IMD brings together executives and professors from all over the world to learn side by side in state-of-the art facilities that have been specially designed for two-way, lead and be led learning.

In this setting, the learning partner participants and the faculty typically discover jointly, through interaction, different approaches and new ways of thinking – with the emphasis increasingly on dilemmas rather than "right" or "wrong" answers. The school's strategic focus is simple enough to allow propositional knowledge to meet prescriptive knowledge. And this specific setting thus provides a strong emphasis on incrementally based research progress!

WORLD-CLASS FACULTY

The HR strategy of any business school should be guided by the continuous striving to deliver even greater academic value. Understanding the school's competence base is key. At IMD, we see the "market" for faculty members as global and open. We feel that we have the freedom to recruit professors from anywhere in the world. Our compensation packages are competitive – a necessary condition, but not enough in itself to attract and retain the best faculty. Although it cannot be quantified, our aim is for every new individual faculty hire to increase the "average" quality level of the faculty team.

More fundamental, of course, will be the faculty's commitment to research-based, practical academic value-creation, along the lines discussed throughout this book. They must see the meaning in these strong institutional values and buy into them. Many academics do!

Our internal organizational structure is simple, which gives IMD the ability to deliver the type of high-impact learning our learning partners expect. As we have seen, there are no academic departments, which means that the teaching and research are typically multidisciplinary and cross-functional. All of our faculty members have the same academic title – professor – and there is no tenure. This, hopefully, provides an incentive for our faculty members to stay relevant, to contribute and to provide value, based on the elimination of all unnecessary committee work – say, for promotion and tenure decisions – a process that can easily eat up faculty time and energy, and create divisiveness and politicking. Faculty members who come to IMD tend to appreciate this. Often they may have even left "comfortable" tenured positions elsewhere, but they enjoy this alternative model of academic value-creation. (On a personal note, let me report that I gave up tenure at Wharton after ten years, and during much of that time, I also held an endowed professorship.)

WORLD-CLASS PARTICIPANTS

Because of its strong relationships in the international business community, IMD is able to attract leading companies and executives, with rich and diverse cultural and experiential backgrounds as learning partners to participate in its programs. As noted, this is particularly important for the research-based academic value-creating process – lead and be led. Top quality professors alone cannot achieve the added relevance and research breakthroughs – the quality of the participants-cum-learning partners must also be top notch. This ensures that the prescriptive knowledge components, so critical for modern academic value-creation and cutting-edge research discovery, are part of the process. The highly qualified, professional field force of corporate development directors (CDDs) works long and hard to identify prospective learning partners, and develop these leads further, and then later acts as a resource for their executive development needs. The same goes for working with specific independent individuals, of course.

TOP-QUALITY CAMPUS AND LEARNING FACILITIES

It is important that a business school's campus is conducive to learning in its broadest sense. The physical arrangements must stimulate learning. In the past, it was perhaps the norm to have horseshoe-shaped auditoria, often with no natural light and with relatively few or no activities going on in study rooms. Today, things are changing significantly: All classrooms must have the latest electronic support equipment, which can often be linked to the study rooms – also well equipped in this regard – so that the work done here can be transferred quickly to the classroom for an enriched learning experience. These group rooms should be large enough to accommodate a maximum of seven to nine people to maximize the give-and-take learning process.

In addition, many of the new classrooms are "flat," so that participants can sit around tables in natural groups. This allows professors to give short "lecturettes," followed by impromptu discussions among the participants gathered around the tables. The outcomes of these discussions are often written on flipcharts, which are then hung along the walls. In short, this fosters a more intensive "action learning" environment.

Typically, all classrooms and study rooms should have high ceilings, with windows to allow natural light in. Even though it has not been scientifically proven, it seems plausible that good learning is associated with high ceilings, i.e. no heavy structure from above "hanging in one's face," potentially cluttering one's mind. Daylight, as well, is probably associated with good learning – we feel that light stimulates a positive mindset and prevents feelings of sluggishness after a day in the classroom. A functional campus, with top notch equipment, support, classrooms and study rooms, along with a meeting place (restaurant) where high quality meals can be enjoyed, seems essential, too, to create the increasingly important atmosphere that is conducive to two-way, interactive learning.

IMD's campus

At IMD we have invested more than CHF 41 million in new physical facilities over the last five years, and the school is about to invest another CHF 34 million in a brand new Learning Center. The campus has thus been entirely transformed over the last five years as follows:

1. *New Executive Learning Center:* 4,200 m², investment CHF 24 million, inaugurated 2002. It contains two large horseshoe-style auditoria, two large "flat rooms" and a third smaller "flat room." In addition, there are forty-nine study rooms.

2. *"The Meeting Place," new dining facility:* 2,150 m², investment CHF 9 million, inaugurated 2005. As in Ancient
Athens, most of the tables are round, to encourage lively
debate among the participants.
3. *The Nestlé Building – New Research and Development
Center:* 1,250 m², investment CHF 8 million, inaugurated
2006. In addition to open-plan office space for more than fifty
research-related staff, the building also houses a large "flat
room" and nine study rooms.
4. *The Maersk McKinney Moller Center:* Due for completion in
June 2008, 5,500 m², anticipated investment CHF 34 million.
It will have eight auditoria, including a large one with seating
for more than 350 participants.

As noted, IMD has no debt. Most of the buildings have been 50
per cent financed by donations from leading individuals and/or
corporations. The remaining 50 per cent has been – or will be –
financed by IMD via its own funds. This signals a partnership
spirit – a willingness for IMD, too, to make commitments, to
take risks, indeed a belief in each project from IMD's side also.
Thus, the financing of the campus expansion has taken place as
a "partnership" between individuals, corporations and IMD. All
entities have shared in the financial burden to make the campus
transition happen.

THE SECRETS OF IMD'S SUCCESS

As we have seen, for a business school to be successful, its strategies
need to have a uniqueness about them that creates value and competitive advantage. At IMD, the combination of four pillars makes our
strategy highly focused and unique:

1. *Real world, real learning:* This implies a practical focus on learning that is founded on thought leadership. Again, this is based on
a heavy emphasis on research and program development, which

presently accounts for 27 per cent of IMD's costs. The speed of transformation from research-based thought leadership to program delivery is also key. Therefore, the pedagogical focus has to be strong. Obviously, IMD's faculty must be of top quality to be able to live up to this first strategic principle – *real* thought leadership for *real*-life situations!

2. *The global meeting place:* IMD attempts to attract executives from all over the world, so that they can learn side by side and so that they can provide their prescriptive inputs in the classroom, based on the best practices of their own company. This sharing of prescriptive best practices benefits all – participants and professors alike. The focus is primarily on critical executive dilemmas, not so much on attempting to find the "right" or "wrong" answers. Cross-cultural insights are vital here. The quality of the participants is thus a must, and this is the cornerstone of IMD's second strategic principle to create a global meeting place.

3. *All learning is lifelong learning:* It is becoming increasingly difficult for executives to take time away from their jobs on an extended basis, although they benefit from coming to IMD to exchange ideas with others and gain a broader perspective on particular challenges that they face. Beyond their participation in programs, executives also need support to practice their lifelong learning back on the job. A weekly webcast helps fulfills this need, supported through a Learning Network membership of approximately 175 companies. Managers in these member companies can participate in the weekly webcasts for free, and so can all IMD alumni. Overall, about 30,000 executives have subscribed for access to the webcasts, with a viewership of up to 3,000 per week! Lifelong learning has thus become an integral part of IMD's strategy.

4. *Minimalist, internal structure and customer focus processes:* A minimalist approach is important so that faculty members can devote most of their energy to research and classroom delivery and not become bogged down in excessive committee work, which can easily lead to time-consuming politicking and meetings. Too

much structure can lead to more emphasis on discipline-based, axiomatic thinking than is desirable, which is probably not consistent with the eclecticism that most leading corporations are looking for in their learning partners.

Strategic pillars one and two reinforce each other – the best of real world, real learning meets the global meeting place; the latest new thoughts from research meet the best of practice as both faculty and participants learn with and from one another. It is a lead and be led value-creation process. Pillars three and four depend on the first two – minimalism in particular is derived from the others, it is a precondition to be able to deliver on them. Thus, IMD's four-pillar strategy is simple enough to be understood by most, to be remembered, to be communicated and, perhaps most important of all, to be inspirational!

Appendix I

The list of publications doing business school rankings is long and the list of the various criteria used in evaluating schools is even longer. The most prominent publications include the *Financial Times*, *Forbes*, *Business Week*, *The Economist Intelligence Unit* and *The Wall Street Journal*. And the criteria used are typically based on some combination of current student surveys, graduating student surveys, alumni surveys, recruiter surveys, data supplied by the schools, research assessments, return on investment for alumni five years after graduation.

To try to make some sense of all this, the *Financial Times* has come up with a methodology to combine the rankings of MBA programs from various publications into one table.

The *Financial Times* also ranks executive education programs. So far, other publications have not yet developed ranking methodologies for such programs. We thus report the *Financial Times* rankings, since a composite ranking is not available for executive programs:

Table A.1 *Global MBA 2007 ranking of rankings[a]*

Global	US	European
1 IMD	1 Columbia Business School	1 IMD
2 Columbia Business School	2 Dartmouth: Tuck	2 London Business School
2 Stanford University GSB	3 University of Chicago GSB	3 Iese Business School
4 London Business School	3 Pennsylvania: Wharton	4 Insead
5 Harvard Business School	5 Harvard Business School	5 Institut de Empresa
5 University of Chicago GSB	5 Stanford University GSB	6 Cambridge: Judge
7 Dartmouth: Tuck	7 Northwestern: Kellogg	7 Esade
8 New York: Stern	8 Michigan: Ross	8 HEC Paris
9 Esade	9 UC Berkeley: Haas	9 SDA Bocconi
9 Iese Business School	10 Yale	10 Cranfield
9 Pennsylvania: Wharton		

[a] The average of the rankings from *Financial Times*, *The Wall Street Journal*, *Business Week*, *Forbes* and *The Economist Intelligence Unit*.

Source: Bradstreet, Della and Wai Kwen Chan, "Global MBA 2007: How the rankings compare: A matter of judgment." *Financial Times*, January 29, 2007.

Table A.2 *Financial Times Executive Education 2007 Combined Rankings for Open Enrollment and Custom Programs*

Rank	School	Custom	Open
1	Duke University: Fuqua & C.E.	1	12
2	Harvard Business School	3	1
3	IMD	2	5
4	University of Chicago GSB	6	4
5	Iese Business School	4	8
6	Babson Executive Education	5	10
7	Center for Creative Leadership	15	6
8	Columbia Business School	7	13
9	Stanford University GSB	26	2
10	Thunderbird School of Global Management	8	15
11	Insead	17	14
11	UCLA: Anderson	20	11
11	University of Virgina: Darden	38	3
14	Ipadc	13	21
14	MIT: Sloan	9	22
14	University of Pennsylvania: Wharton	17	18
17	HEC Paris	11	27
17	London Business School	22	20
17	University of Western Ontario: Ivey	23	18
20	Fundação Dom Cabral	27	17

This table is compiled from the scores underlying the Financial Times Executive Education 2007 open-enrollment program and custom program rankings. Both sets of data are given equal weight, but the overall result is not equal to the average of the two printed figures for each school.

Source: "Financial Times Executive Education 2007." *Financial Times,* May 14, 2007.

Appendix II

CORE REFERENCES
Publications authored by Peter Lorange:

"A performance-based, minimalist human resource management approach in business schools," *Human Resource Management* 45 (Winter 2006), 649–658.

> This article focuses on the need for top-quality professors in business schools and how their drive for enhancing academic value-creation, generating cutting-edge research, leading teaching and building strong interrelationships with students and executive participants fuels the success of the academic institution. Obviously, the administration is also important and must be outstanding, along with the research associates, finance staff, marketing team and the like. Still, in order to contribute to the overall success of the academic institution, these other functions all depend on an outstanding professorial staff – they cannot create success alone.

"Strategy means choice: Also for today's business school!," *Journal of Management Development* 24 (2005), 783–790.

> Drawing on IMD's experience and strategy, implicitly and explicitly, this article reports on unique, new thinking on strategy-setting and key priorities for business schools and academic institutions.

"The marketing of market-based value creation in today's business schools," *International Journal of Marketing Education* 1 (2005), 35–44.

This article explores how marketing, as part of a business school's value creation, is now more central than ever, and it requires a fundamentally different focus in light of the network marketing challenges that are being created as part of today's knowledge society.

"Scripting a CEO roundtable," in P. Strebel and T. Keys (eds.), *Mastering executive education: How to combine content with context and emotion – The IMD guide* (Harlow: FT Prentice Hall, 2004), 345–352.

This chapter discusses how a CEO roundtable can be run to achieve valuable take-home benefits for the participants, value creation in terms of relationship building for the host organization, as well as value for each keynote speaker who has specific inputs.

"Complex collaboration: The case of a business school and its complex network of relationships," in M. M. Beyerlin, D. A. Johnson and S. T. Beyerlin (eds.), *Complex collaboration: Building the capabilities for working across boundaries* (Amsterdam: Elsevier, 2004), 109–124.

This chapter argues that complex collaborations and networks with both leading corporations and other academic institutions will be necessary for the modern business school to grow and to distance itself from commoditization.

"Developing global leaders," *BizEd*, AACSB International (September/ October 2003), 24–27.

Using examples from IMD, this article posits that the central challenge for management educators is to design a multifaceted, comprehensive approach to global business education, while encompassing the different cultural perspectives of the students. Business schools must offer executive programs that focus on the issues of globalization, without teaching any one prescribed approach to those issues.

"Global responsibility – business education and business schools – roles in promoting a global perspective," *International Journal of Business in Society* 3 (2003), 126–135.

> This article is based on the author's experience as head of a leading international business school, with strong embedded values in providing the highest level of quality business education within a global perspective. The article concludes with a discussion regarding an optimal location for the global business school. It is argued that perhaps many of today's leading business schools, being located in major markets, will not have an optimal location because these major markets can more or less explicitly lead to a nationally based bias of the teaching and research being undertaken.

"Leadership challenges in leading business schools," in E. De Corte (ed.), *Excellence in higher education, Wenner-Gren International Series*, volume 82 (London: Portland Press, 2003), 141–157.

> Excellence, when it comes to academic value-creation in business schools, is becoming more of a must in today's brain-driven, networked-based society. This chapter focuses on how this can be achieved with a balanced portfolio of activities – based on the considerations of market forces and the vision of the school's leadership.

"The industry view of collaborative research," in W. Z. Hirsch and L. Weber (eds.), *As the walls of academia are tumbling down* (London: Economica, 2002), 175–187.

> In this chapter, a conceptual framework is put forward on how collaboration between academia and industry can enhance internally generated growth. Additionally, six specific challenges regarding collaborative research are addressed and the ideal conditions for success are outlined.

"Business education: opportunity – and a threat – corporate universities and business schools can learn to cohabit," *Financial Times* (March 26, 2001).

> This article discusses the emergence of corporate universities, the possible threats they pose to business schools and how they can create win-win situations by building on their complementarities.

"Setting strategic direction in academic institutions: How do school leaders find the means to lead?," *efmd Forum* 1 (2001), 9–16.

> In this article, four approaches to strategy in business schools are proposed in order to ensure that the main missions – research, teaching and citizenship – of the school are operationally carried out.

and Xavier Gilbert, "The difference between teaching and learning," *EBF* 7 (Autumn 2001), 7–8.

> This article addresses how executives learn and the four ways that third parties can be really helpful to the "learning executive" – 1) Place an emphasis on learning how to learn, 2) develop a real learning partnership ideally between the business school and the company, 3) leverage executive-to-executive learning and 4) provide an action learning context.

"A business school as a learning organization," *The Learning Organization* 3 (1996), 5–13.

> This article examines the concept of a business school as a learning organization. It discusses the issue of change as a stimulus for learning, proposes the idea of the faculty member as the learner, as well as the integration of various modes of organizational learning. It illustrates a working model for organizational learning comprised of learning from research activities, workshops, open teaching programs as well as in-company tailored programs. The article concludes with an emphasis on partnerships with

multinational cutting-edge firms as the key to the most relevant real-life organizational learning.

"Future of management education," in M. Warner (ed.), *International encyclopedia of business and management*, volume 3 (London: Routledge, 1996), 2724–2734.

This chapter examines the future of management education from a strategic point of view. It offers an appraisal of those factors most likely to have the largest impact on management education, explores differences between European and US management education, looks at the most important trends in the marketplace and provides the basis for a strategic prescription for the future.

Index

communication tools, development of
   new 112
competition, in face of 103–4
effective, key factors 111–12
excitement of organization, need to
   reflect 93
messages, mix of, need to understand
   101
messages, need for clarity 103
minimalistic, trend towards 94
mix, advertising in, ineffectiveness of
   91
mix, website as critical aspect 90
outside-in approach, friction from 96
propositions to guide, five strategic
   92–5
relationship, importance of 90
see also relationship marketing
strategy 91–117
   interactive process as key theme of
      95
   need for simple strategic
      propositions 102
   success, alumni links with, as key 94
   team, essential for emphasizing trade-
      offs 104
   willingness to invest in 94
Maznevski, Martha 168
MBA
   diary 107
   market fluctuations 192
   program, marketing, differing from
      EMBA 116
   programs 46–50
      IMD's 48–50
      market shifts 46
Meehan, S. 8
meeting place, importance of metaphor of 27
Mintzberg, H. 47, 195
MIT 18
   links with IMD 198
Mokyr, Joel 5
Mokyr's proposition 7
Mumbai Research Centre 73, 78–9
   India-in-the-World based research 195
"Must Win Battles" approach 25, 73
Muzyka, Daniel 105–6

Nestlé, learning partners strategy 176–7
Nissan 179

O'Toole, J. 210
one-team culture, as citizenship 145
open-enrollment programs 36–41
   active management, need for 40
   constant renewal, need for 40
   model of marketing challenge *102*
   thought leadership in 40
open executive programs, source of
      interaction between research
      and practice 35
opportunities, development, from real life 1
Orchestrating Winning Performance
      Program (OWP), *see* IMD, OWP
organizational form, US-based, viable
      alternative to 12
organizational structure, minimalist,
      features of 152

participants, importance of top-caliber 62
partnerships, learning, importance of full-
      blown 124
   see also learning partner; learning
      partnership
Perspectives for Managers 52
podcasts, as means of intensifying
      dissemination 51
Porter, Michael 5
portfolio, diversified, risks of 196
prescriptive knowledge 1
Proctor & Gamble 3
procurement, risks of dominant cost focus
      174
product
   cutting edge, need for 97
   innovations, from interaction with lead
      customers 7
professionals, as core community 100
professors
   link with program participants 144
   performance, new criteria for judging
      144
   prior preparation by joining 43
   recruit from anywhere, freedom to
      151–2
   thought leadership, ready to expose to
      best practice 142
   see also faculty
program
   design, eclectic, key to MBA programs 7
   development, inside-out approach 91